Surviving Female Friendships

The Good, The Bad, and The Ugly

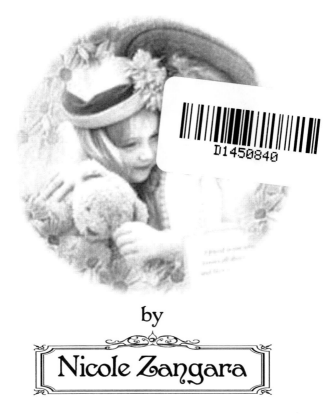

D1450840

by

Nicole Zangara

Published by
Brighton Publishing LLC
501 W. Ray Road
Suite 4
Chandler, Arizona 85225

Surviving Female Friendships
The Good, The Bad, and The Ugly

by

Nicole Zangara

Published by
Brighton Publishing LLC
501 W. Ray Road
Suite 4
Chandler, Arizona 85225
BrightonPublishing.com

Copyright © 2012

ISBN 13: 978-1-621830-11-5
ISBN 10: 1-621830-11-X

Printed in the United States of America

First Edition

Cover Design By: Tom Rodriguez

❧ Dedication ❧

To the two people I admire most: my parents. Thank you for always believing in me and, therefore, giving me a reason to believe in myself.

Nicole Zangara

෨ Acknowledgements ଷ

*T*hanks first and foremost to my wonderful publisher, Kathie McGuire. This book would not have been possible if not for you and your fabulous team at Brighton Publishing. Thank you for taking a chance on me; you've helped to make one of my dreams a reality.

I'm honored to recognize the woman who gave me the push I needed to write this book, Cathy Binstock. Your encouragement, guidance, and friendship will never be forgotten.

To all of the brave and inspirational women who shared their friendship stories, I'm beyond grateful to each and every one of you.

And last but not least, a huge thanks to my family. I'm unbelievably lucky to be related to such loving, warm, and amazing people who remind me not to take life too seriously. My brothers, Jeremy and Ryan, whom I adore more than they know yet will continue to annoy (I am your little sister!); my mother Donna, for always keeping me grounded and for being the woman I have looked up to since I was a little girl; I will forever be your fraughter (friend+daughter); my father Richard, whom I deeply respect and appreciate for all he has taught and continues to teach me, as well as for enduring those long road trips that brought us closer together; my sister-in-law Betsy, whom I consider to be the sister I never had and always wanted; and finally to my grandmother Rose, who will forever have a special place in my heart.

℘ Prologue ℘

J began this journey intending to explore friendships among single women in their twenties and thirties, and intended to use my own experiences as a basis for my work. However, it soon dawned on me that this book could be helpful to women of any age. When discussing this concept with women of various ages, I heard their difficult experiences with same-sex friendships. Women in their forties, fifties, and sixties recounted stories that left me feeling more confused about female friendships. Some stories were painful, out of the ordinary, and heartbreaking—while others left me stumped because there was no logical reason for the relationship to end.

So my route changed, taking me down paths that ultimately led to not only writing about my own experiences, but also including a collection of stories, thoughts, and experiences from women ranging in ages from twenty to sixty-plus—although all the names, locations, and details have been changed for anonymity. Storytelling can have a major and lasting impact, and individuals can relate to and find validation in others' experiences. These stories offer the reader real-life examples and widen the book's usefulness, as well as provide comfort in knowing that you're not alone. I also enjoy telling stories, as well as listening to them; and I hope you'll enjoy reading the ones recounted here.

I feel there are insufficient resources available to help women who are going through complex female friendship experiences. The currently popular milieus of social media and technology are leading to new, more challenging, and more frequent encounters which, in turn, require new interpersonal strategies.

The experiences I refer to concern not only friendships between and among women, but also how utterly confusing these relationships can be—especially as we age and/or enter into more committed friendships and attachments. I do not intend to pass on newfound wisdom, but rather to examine everyday experiences with friends that are difficult, as well as ones that make us ask out loud, "Really? Did that just happen?" I've often imagined creating a *Saturday Night Live* skit using my everyday experiences. It's important to laugh—because sometimes laughing is all we can do.

Surviving Female Friendships: The Good, The Bad, and The Ugly
~ Nicole Zangara

My goal is that you will be challenged to look at people around you—as well as at yourself—and reflect on these relationships. My hope is that you'll take comfort in knowing that we all have been through trying times with friends and there's no right or wrong way to manage them. It can only be helpful to openly acknowledge and discuss these situations, and to know they happen to every woman, at every age.

ஐ Chapter One ௧

Females: Can't Live With Them, Can't Live Without Them

Some say our experiences define us; others say we create our own destiny. I fall somewhere in the middle. I believe the events we experience shape our framework for and outlook on life. These situations affect how we feel, think, and act toward others. On the other hand, I'm a firm believer in taking action to obtain a desired outcome, even when the odds are against you.

So what does all this talk have to do with female friendships? Plenty! Over the years, I've experienced both positive and negative female friendships. I'm human, which means I have thoughts and feelings, I'm sensitive and can be easily hurt, and that words can impact me powerfully. I believe many of my friendships with women have helped me to become who I am today because they have caused me to reflect on and be curious about what went wrong and what went right.

Lisa, a friend from graduate school who I feel is wise and intelligent beyond her thirty-some years, e-mailed me with advice about a situation with another friend. After offering wonderful and useful advice, Lisa said that I wasn't the only one going through such struggles and I wasn't special in that regard. After I got over the cold, hard truth of her statement, I realized how accurate and insightful it was.

These experiences happen to women of all ages. Every woman has a story, and these accounts, even when difficult, emotional, or heartbreaking, offer insight into our own plights. So I'm telling my story and sharing others' in the hope that it'll help all of us understand that female friendships are tough—and there's no single or easy way to navigate them. So let's start from the beginning.

Girls can be mean; girls can be cruel. Rent *Mean Girls*, watch it, and tell me there's not some truth about childhood and adolescent friendships in that movie. There's something about women's relationships that bring out jealousy and competition. Why? Because many of us are taught, and/or expected, to be successful while also being pretty, fit, soft-spoken, sweet, and so on. We're taught, implicitly and explicitly, to act a certain way in society. So when we feel threatened by another female, something is triggered within us and we become a whole new person—sometimes one with claws unsheathed.

Surviving Female Friendships: The Good, The Bad, and The Ugly
~ Nicole Zangara

Women who are strong are often incorrectly seen as She Devils, while men who are strong are seen as powerful. I am not writing this book to hate on men (I'm a heterosexual female and respect men), but when looking at female friendships, one must look at the differences between the sexes, what women are already dealing with, and what we bring to the friendship.

Females can be complicated to have as friends because we're (sorry, here comes a stereotype and generalization) more in touch with our feelings, and so we're able to access and use them more easily. Women have the ability to be nurturing, as well as the ability to be vicious and cold. Have you ever had a fight with a good friend and suddenly find her distant and not the nice friend she used to be? In a matter of minutes, you may become afraid of what she will say or do, which can be scary.

Unfortunately, fear is a common feeling we experience in our friendships, and one that we don't talk about because no woman wants to tell a friend that she's afraid of her. Why are we so apprehensive about discussing this with one another? It seems women don't want to acknowledge that there's some doubt about the friendship; or maybe that you don't know your friend as well as you thought, especially after having some type of disagreement.

3

Surviving Female Friendships: The Good, The Bad, and The Ugly
~ Nicole Zangara

In the face of conflict, we see the real person, and sometimes she can be downright ugly. Some women believe that if they ignore the feeling, it'll go away, meaning that the friend will forget about the fight you had and go back to being her normal, nice self, instead of confronting the issue.

In addition, letting a friend know we're afraid shows that we're vulnerable, which opens us up to possible judgment and criticism. Let's be honest and say we don't want that to happen. We can never be sure that a friend, no matter how close she may be, will accept our insecurities and not tell us we're wrong or stupid for feeling that way. Fear can be debilitating in friendships, and this is something I address in these findings.

Have you ever told your best friend about someone at work who is being mean to you, and the friend becomes super-protective and jokingly makes comments about prank-calling that person? We want to let our friends know that we'll fight for them, that we'll beat up their enemy, even if that person is six foot two and weighs twice what we do. However, when there is conflict in a friendship, we tap into our emotions which can overpower us and lead us to say or do things we wouldn't normally say or do.

Where there are two female friends, there will be drama and issues. I don't watch *The Real Housewives* series, but for those who do, I'm sure you understand. We get territorial about our friendships and form strong attachments that aren't easy to break.

I've had many discussions with friends who've had difficulties managing their relationships with other women. I often wonder why this is so, and why men don't ponder their male friendships over bowls of ice cream and bars of chocolate. But men are usually not as emotionally connected in their friendships. There are exceptions, but men generally have different types of attachments than women. Again, this is stereotypical, but men bond differently and engage in less emotionally charged activities, such as going to sporting events or working out together. They share the experience of the activity, whereas women share the experience on a deeper emotional level.

Men's communication is also more action-driven. Have you ever had a conversation with a male about an issue you're having and, instead of listening, he wanted to fix the problem? Generally speaking, men are fixers and doers; they discuss facts, while women discuss emotions, opinions, and details. If you disagree with this assessment, ask the nearest male how he's doing or how his day is going. I'm fairly confident you'll get a fifteen-second answer. Then go ask the nearest female the same question. You may want to grab a bag of popcorn on your way.

Women have an emotional intensity unlike men's. When we hear that our best friend is hurting—maybe going through a divorce or caring for a sick parent—we feel for her, and may walk through the process with her. For example, to alleviate her stress, we may offer to help out with her children. We invest our time because we care about the friendship. I'm not saying that men don't feel or react to their emotions, but women tend to have a greater emotional spectrum than men, and those feelings can lead to deeper connections.

Females lean on each other, and will go get Oreos at two o'clock in the morning after a fight with a boyfriend. Women share intimate details and feelings with each other. They think about what they'll wear on a date, and will call their best friend to go through different outfits in detail, including the accessories and makeup. And that same person will call after the date to relate the play-by-play—who said what, what it meant, and how the guy had salad in his teeth but it was the most adorable thing ever. Men don't typically do this; women, however, do—and these meaningful experiences and connections can lead to heartbreaking friendship breakups.

Surviving Female Friendships: The Good, The Bad, and The Ugly
~ Nicole Zangara

This is why I feel this issue needs to be documented and discussed. Because of our innate need for deep, genuine bonds, when something goes haywire it can be extremely difficult to process. Roses may be red and violets may be blue, but sometimes we just cannot stand being friends with other females, and that's okay.

Friendships are undeniably complex, and women are complicated beings. Thus, having and maintaining female attachments can be challenging, especially when there is intense emotion, drama, different points of view, and the drifting apart that can happen with age. However, female friendship can be a wonderful union that provides strength, love, and comfort.

I wish to examine all aspects of female friendships— the good, the bad, and the ugly. And especially the ones that shift with no rhyme or reason, the ones that fizzle out without explanation, the ones that make us question why we were friends in the first place, and the ones that make us realize we can't stand some of the relationships. This book is meant to help you look at these experiences and say, "Hey, sometimes these things happen, and you've gotta go with it." So sit down, pour a glass of wine, and get ready to dive in.

Victoria: A Woman in Her 60s

Victoria takes a lot of pride in having great female friendships, and she has many wonderful, longtime friends to prove it. She values her friendships and knows how important it is to have a positive support system. Anytime things seem to change in her relationships, she immediately addresses the issue so she and her friend can work through it. Part of this is due to her no-nonsense personality, but another part is due to the fact that Victoria doesn't like to let problems linger. However, like so many women, she has been in more than one situation where she was unsuccessful in her attempts to repair a friendship.

About twenty years ago, Victoria and Sally were close friends who had much in common; they had similar religious backgrounds, were married to men in the same profession, and both had twins. They enjoyed spending time with one another and with each other's families. They shared many wonderful moments, and Victoria felt she had a close bond with Sally. However, without explanation, something changed. Victoria attempted to address the issue in several ways; she even spoke to Sally's husband, who assured her nothing was wrong. But Victoria still has no idea what happened and still feels confused. The two see each other occasionally, but never speak. Victoria has had a difficult time forgetting this friendship, and has learned that sometimes things cannot be worked out. This has not been an easy thing for her to accept.

Victoria had a similar experience with Tina, a woman she met through her children's school about twenty-five years ago. Victoria instantly felt close to Tina, and they began to spend a lot of time together—partly due to the fact that Victoria was working part-time and Tina was a stay-at-home mom. However, as Victoria's work schedule increased and she made more friends, Tina seemed to become envious.

Over the years, Victoria watched the friendship change as a result of Tina's jealousy, and noticed that Tina's behavior had become controlling, which didn't sit well with her. As in the previous situation, Victoria attempted to address the issue, but without success. The issues became overwhelming and negatively impacted the friendship. Also, Victoria and Tina's husbands were close friends and their relationship was affected to the point that they, too, were unable to continue their friendship. This is not uncommon when married women breakup with their friends.

Conflict or tension between individuals in groups of friends can lead to friendship breakups. Victoria experienced

9

this about eighteen years ago when her children were playing sports. Like many parents who have active children, Victoria met a group of women through these events and spent countless nights and weekends with them; however, there seemed to be tension with Rebecca. Because of this, Victoria made a conscious decision to not spend time with her; in addition, as Victoria's children became older, they spent less time with Rebecca's children, which decreased the necessity of spending time with her. Victoria felt no great loss, but this is an interesting example of what can take place when women in a group stop putting effort into a friendship.

ഇ Chapter Two രെ

History: How It All Began

I have both positive and negative memories of female friends from my childhood. For example, I have wonderful memories of sleep-away camp, which I attended from ages ten to fifteen. I become nostalgic for those days every summer, remembering the remarkable experiences I had during those eight weeks. I cherish those days because my friendships were so innocent and tender. I learned a lot about the intense female bond, and what it means to live with a group of females. My camp friends became my best friends, and I felt very close to them; even without having stayed in regular contact for ten-plus years, they remain in my heart. We fought, we laughed, we talked about boys, and it was the highlight of my summer—childhood at its best.

11

Surviving Female Friendships: The Good, The Bad, and The Ugly
~ Nicole Zangara

I also remember fun-filled birthday parties, play dates, and hanging out with my friends, as well as getting sand put in my hair and being made fun of for having braces and wearing glasses. I will not whine or complain about these experiences because, as my friend Lisa says, we all go through them. My downfall, though, was that I wanted to be the popular kid, so I tried to hang out with the popular kids even when I knew it was dumb. But there was something so enticing about sitting at the popular kids' lunch table, or just standing next to others who were known as the cool kids. Of course, I now look back and think how ridiculous I was, especially since the popular kids were not nice; come to think of it, they were fairly cruel. But I was thirteen years old and everything seemed so important. I was also boy crazy, and the popular boys only looked at the popular girls, so that added to my desire.

Thankfully, I had a time-consuming extracurricular activity that took up most of my free time—dance. I danced—tap, jazz, ballet, and hip-hop—for fifteen years, and absolutely loved it. (Tap was and always will be my favorite, because some steps are incredibly tricky. Once I got them, it felt like a major accomplishment.) Over those fifteen years, dance became not just an identity, but also an integral part of my life.

Surviving Female Friendships: The Good, The Bad, and The Ugly
~ Nicole Zangara

Dancing taught me self-confidence, poise, and how to use my body as a form of self-expression. I learned to connect with my dance peers, male and female, in a way that helped me to become more self-assured, and to also seek out the same type of person in school and create healthy female attachments. In many ways, I believe that dancing saved me, because I became a leader instead of a follower. Moreover, dancing allowed me to develop my own personality rather than the cool kid identity. Through dance, I learned that I was really good at something, and that I didn't need the validation of others to feel good about myself. Dancing gave me the tools I needed to succeed and know that I could do something if I put my mind and body toward my goals. I also became competitive. Maybe I always was, but dancing brought out that trait and helped me out of my cocoon. I felt incredibly powerful and energized on stage, and I knew that I was thoroughly enjoying my hard work and dedication with each show.

In high school, it would be safe to say that I had a fairly normal experience; I was consumed with schoolwork, extra-curricular activities, and trying to fit in with various groups of friends. I was more concerned about getting into a good college and getting my homework done than about being considered popular. Finding high-quality and like-minded friends was difficult, yet I ended up doing okay. I liked to hang out with different people, so I was never in only one clique or group. I guess you could say I was a floater, which has persisted into adulthood; I prefer not being labeled in one way. Maybe it's my rebellion against labels.

As a teenager, I was also close to my parents and had an open and honest relationship with them. I never had a curfew; I never was grounded. I was a fairly good kid who was too scared to do anything wrong. Looking back, I'm grateful for my family's support—especially my mother's—as I tried to navigate adolescence and early adulthood. I was able to talk openly with her about my feelings, which helped me immensely. I am still thankful for the continued support my parents provide.

A fond memory I have from high school, which I will never forget, is of a friend who taught me the true meaning of "actions speak louder than words." When I found out I didn't get into the college of my choice, I was devastated and spent the entire day on my living room couch, crying. I thought my life was over, felt like a complete failure, and was disappointed in myself. I decided to walk to the mailbox, as that had become my daily routine when waiting for acceptance/rejection letters from colleges. When I opened it, I saw a card from my friend Gina.

Surviving Female Friendships: The Good, The Bad, and The Ugly
~ Nicole Zangara

We were close friends, and she was someone I considered a best friend throughout high school. She even came to my last dance recital during our senior year; I got her a ticket in the front row next to my parents and saw her sitting there during my performance—which meant a lot. We would go out to eat, watch *Dawson's Creek*, and talk on the phone regularly. She was always calm and mature, which helped me because I wasn't always calm!

Suffice it to say, Gina knew how much I'd wanted to get into this particular college, so when I took her card out of the mailbox and read it, I was touched by her effort to make me feel better. It read:

Nicole,

I thought you could use some encouragement today. I want you to know that even if college admissions people don't recognize what they are missing, I know what they are. I'm so proud of you for everything you have done since the beginning of high school. For how far you have come as a person, as a student, and as a dancer. I'm proud of how no matter what obstacles got in your way, you always kept trying. Right now it may seem like all your efforts did not pay off. But they did. You have developed work habits and dedication that will last you through college and beyond. All colleges have something to offer you and you will meet amazing people wherever you go. Try to remain optimistic, I know people who love their school even though they didn't love it when they looked at it. College is college and it's out of this town (smiley face). Smile. And I'm calling you later today to see if you still want to go out tonight. I hope you do.

Love,

Gina

This kind act meant more to me than Gina will ever know, and it showed me how deep our friendship was. I was still upset, but it helped to have a friend in my corner. It was at this moment that I learned that actions have the greatest impact and leave lasting impressions. I appreciate Gina even now, because she took the time to think about me during that upsetting episode. She made my life a little more bearable, and it helped to know I wasn't alone. I've held onto this letter for the past ten years to remind myself that there are good people out there; they're just one in a million.

It would be safe to assume that we all went through high school having had differing levels of experiences with friends, some positive and some negative; some people were

Surviving Female Friendships: The Good, The Bad, and The Ugly
~ Nicole Zangara

popular and had many friends, while other people did not. Our hormones, self-esteem, and ever-changing moods influenced our relationships, and I found that, each year, I looked for—and made—more mature friendships. As I became more secure, I began looking for others who also felt the same. As I look back, I realize I've always been drawn to older people and have had older friends. I've also enjoyed being around people who seemed to have their act together and felt confident and good about themselves. I believe they had a positive influence on me during my transition into college.

There, it was quite simple to make friends because of the number of people around; there were people with common interests; and it was easier to get together when you could simply walk across the hall. The accessibility factor is the key because it allows for expanded social experiences and opportunities.

College was incredible because I love learning and being intellectually stimulated, and I enjoy meeting all sorts of people. However, I had a painful experience that seems to be quite common among females. I joined a sorority during my freshman year and loved it. The first year was wonderful; I was excited to be welcomed into a circle of women who seemed to genuinely care. I felt connected not only to my

17

recruitment class, but also to the class a year ahead of me. I felt I was part of a family and there was a sense of home and belonging.

During that first year, I had many positive experiences; going to fun social events and spending time getting to know some fascinating women. There were a few sisters a year older than me who also lived on the same floor of the dorm, and it was enjoyable to stop by and chat. I thoroughly treasured those times and feel they enhanced my college experience.

However (you knew this was coming), after living with some of my sisters and experiencing college life, it became apparent that I wasn't fitting in as well as I'd thought. I began to feel disconnected. I rarely drank alcohol, which put me in a different category. I never felt pressured to drink, but it was made fun of or commented on in some way if I didn't. I learned to bring a cup to events so people would assume I was drinking alcohol instead of Diet Coke. I felt stupid inside, but it worked, and people were more accepting.

After some time, I felt I didn't have the same interests and values as others in the sorority. Sometimes I'd have a discussion with a sister who had an opinion unlike mine, and it didn't seem to be okay that we had differences. I also didn't enjoy the partying scene, which was a common interest I didn't share. In addition, I was becoming more focused on my studies and started to turn my attention to my plans for internships, as well as long-term plans for graduate school. It was obvious I was going down a different path, and it didn't take long for me to start feeling uneasy about the friendships.

Looking back, I can't pinpoint a single incident that led me to feel this way; it was a combination of events and interactions which left me feeling uncomfortable and as if I couldn't be myself. I also felt the friendships were not as genuine as they'd seemed, and began to struggle with them. For example, while living with some of the women, I saw how they really were, and I didn't like it nor did I like the way I was being treated. This was especially true of some of the women in my class; I felt we weren't on the same page anymore and that they really didn't know me. Maybe that wasn't true, but I didn't feel a connection or anything beyond the superficial. I started contemplating the idea to resign my membership.

You may be wondering if I spoke up or tried to change things before I made a decision. I did not. However, as is true of any issue in a friendship, nothing is clear-cut because there are so many layers of emotions. It was twofold; on one hand, I see my early twenty-something self—too timid to share her feelings and not knowing how to begin such a discussion, and felt I'd be ostracized or made fun of. On the other hand, I was past the point of reconciliation and, therefore, done. I've often remarked that for a friendship to survive, both parties must want it to succeed. I'd lost that motivation.

As all this was happening, I left to spend a semester abroad in Sydney, Australia. I thought this would give me the space and time I needed to make a decision regarding whether I would stay in the sorority. Going abroad taught me independence and I learned that I could start fresh. It also showed me what true friendships looked and felt like at a time when I wasn't sure anymore.

During those months, I met the most caring, warm women. When I found out I was assigned to live on the all-girls' floor of the dorm, my first reaction was, "Oh great, more female drama!" But it was just the opposite. One of the women, Stella, taught me how to be more patient and giving, as well as how to discuss my feelings—even when they differed from hers. She showed me how accepting a friend can be regardless of your views. I also learned about different cultures and beliefs, since many of the women there came from all around the world.

Surviving Female Friendships: The Good, The Bad, and The Ugly
~ Nicole Zangara

So there I was, in Australia, feeling respected and accepted by women who'd been raised with a completely different set of values, yet I didn't feel the same connection with women back home, with whom I shared somewhat similar backgrounds. Needless to say, it was a major awakening to whom I was surrounding myself with at college.

I'm incredibly grateful for the friendships I made in Australia, and how comfortable I felt around those inspiring women. I left Australia a better person, and knew the decision I would make when I returned; I had to resign my sorority membership and I knew it was going to suck. And when I returned for my senior year, that was what I did.

It may not seem like a big deal, but at the time it felt like it was. I was leaving a sisterhood that had influenced my friendships, my social life, and my college experience; walking away from that was incredibly difficult. And, as a senior, I had to find a new niche for myself, which was challenging. I was breaking up with and leaving the life I'd created at college.

The process of resigning was very much like a bad breakup. I had to give back sorority memorabilia; I had to sit down with chapter members to discuss what had happened. And there were multiple breakups with people involved in the sorority. It was humiliating, weird, and all of the other emotions that accompany a breakup.

I also had to come up with a reason why I'd resigned. I wrote a letter for the chapter president to read at the next meeting as a way of getting my voice heard. I wanted a part of me to be there to say that I felt hurt and disconnected, and to say a proper goodbye. I've always wondered how the members interpreted my words. In a way, I wanted to stick it out and graduate with my recruitment class, but I felt I wouldn't be true to myself if I remained in an organization in which I felt disparaged. I had to listen to myself and my feelings, and acknowledge that I couldn't stand being friends with certain people in the sorority because I'd seen their real selves and didn't want to associate with them. This wasn't easy to do, because who wants to openly admit that she doesn't get along with others?

After I resigned, it was even more painful to see who stopped talking to me and how quickly it happened. Even those women who I thought had my back and were supportive of my decision to resign my membership slowly stopped socializing with me. It was awful, yet it confirmed and validated how I was feeling. Of course, there were positive results as well. I was able to make new friends and work on my non-sorority friendships. And there were those sorority sisters who remained my friends; now I realize how difficult it must have been for them to do so because of the way I resigned. I imagine that I wasn't discussed favorably among the women, and so whoever still associated with me must have received some remarks. That may be my insecurities talking, but it's hard to believe that my decision to leave the sorority didn't cause some ill feelings or gossip. We're talking about women!

Another positive that came out of my decision was that I focused on myself—academically and creatively. I started to plan my future and decided what graduate school program I wanted to apply to. I also took voice lessons, as I'd always been interested in singing. I'm not sure I was all that good, but for one afternoon a week, it was pleasurable to learn how to sing and feel I'd accomplished something for me.

I often wonder if I made a silly decision and created drama; I'm still not sure. I look at the positive and the negative results of that choice—standing up for myself, yet leaving an organization I believed in. I took the path less chosen and, after discussing my experiences, have heard similar stories. And so, again, I'm not special in terms of what I went through. However, this episode shaped the way I value friendships and caused me to reflect on the person I am, as well as the type of person I want to have as a friend.

The hardest part of this process was telling those sisters I did care about, including those in the classes above and below mine, and who had nothing to do with my resignation. I knew that no reason I gave would make sense or alleviate their feelings. Many of these women had positive experiences and relationships in the sorority, so my choice was considered extreme.

However, I knew this decision was about making me feel better, not about trying to make someone else feel better. That may sound selfish, but I was done avoiding my feelings, and I needed to acknowledge that and do something about it. Thankfully, I've now reconnected with a few of these women and I'm glad we're friends; and not just because we were in the same organization and we should be friends. The friendship's foundation is built on a different set of values, including trust and respect.

In graduate school, especially in the school of social work, it was more difficult to make friends due to the age range of my fellow students. Many were women in their mid- to late-forties or fifties who were either stay-at-home mothers or women seeking a career change. Living off-campus also limited my access to social opportunities.

Surviving Female Friendships: The Good, The Bad, and The Ugly
~ Nicole Zangara

One has numerous roles and responsibilities as a graduate student. Graduate school is much more serious than undergraduate. This could be due to age and maturity as well as the focus on career rather than on extracurricular activities. In addition, there are significant life questions. What will it be like to enter the real world after I graduate? How will I pay off these loans? What do I really want to do with my life?

Graduate school kept me busy with practicums, schoolwork, and my caseload; so being social all the time was not my first priority. I ended up having a few close friends who were all I needed during those two years.

When I graduated, I moved to a new city for a postgraduate fellowship in clinical social work. At first, it was difficult to find people who had the same interests; but I was lucky enough to have a college friend nearby who introduced me to her friends, so I had an easier time finding my niche. Interestingly, Michelle was in the same sorority, but a year older, and we'd stayed in contact somewhat throughout the years. I'd met her at my first college party during freshman year; she'd always been a warm and inviting person who took me under her wing. I also met people through my job, as well through alumni gatherings and other social events.

Surviving Female Friendships: The Good, The Bad, and The Ugly
~ Nicole Zangara

As I get older, it seems more difficult to find people I consider true friends. As we mature, we become more serious about our friendships, just as we become more serious about our careers. There's a desire to be around people who are reliable and trustworthy; since we no longer rely on our parents as much, our friends become our go-to for support and comfort. Just as in a romantic relationship, we want friends who will be there when the going gets rough.

Also, as we grow older, we begin to lose touch with old friends—part of the natural progression of moving on with our lives. We live in a world where people often change location; and frequently, we likely have friends in many places. Those who still talk to childhood friends regularly are the exception. It amazes me when I hear that some people still talk to their elementary school friends. I have a difficult time understanding how people maintain such long-lasting friendships, perhaps because that part of my life seems so far away or perhaps it's due to the fact that I no longer live in the state where I grew up and rarely keep in touch with those childhood friends.

When two people live in different cities or states, it takes extra effort to maintain a friendship—more phone calls, e-mails, texts, and letters, as well as scheduling visits for major life events, such as weddings and/or baby showers. If both people are invested, the effort is well worth it; however, if one person stops responding or communication decreases, something is going on that should be addressed.

I think it's considered taboo to have this discussion—the one where you and your friend discuss your friendship and where it stands, as well as how you're both feeling about it—as it's considered complaining or overly dramatic. Women already have a reputation for being too emotional and over-analyzing things, especially when it comes to relationships and social experiences. However, I challenge you to get a bunch of your girlfriends together and ask them about their past and present friendship experiences. It's not openly talked about or acknowledged that women (sorry, men, I can't write for you) have a difficult time navigating relationships—personal or platonic—as we age. This topic deserves more attention; especially as we look at ourselves, the types of people we attract and are attracted to, and who we want in our lives. Looking at our friends provides insight into who we are.

I believe that there are many different reasons why some friendships survive while others don't. I feel lucky that I've experienced a few incredible friendships over the years; from sleep-away camp to the present day, I can confidently say that I'm continuing to learn about the complexity of female friendships. Even after my experience in the sorority, I still believe in the power of the female bond. Going to Australia allowed me to grow and understand myself and what I needed in a friendship. Since then, I've experienced enough interactions to know that they come in all shapes and sizes.

Friendships are amazing and important because they provide positive things that our parents, siblings and/or significant others cannot provide. Friendships help keep us stable and sane in an unstable, crazy world. When something good happens, we want to call a friend and share the news; when we need to vent or discuss how horrible we're feeling, a good friend can provide support and comfort. However, friendships are like a roller coaster ride: they go up, they go down, and you sometimes just have to enjoy the ride.

Callie: A Woman in Her 50s

Ever since Callie can remember, she has always had at least one close female friend. Her first best friend was her childhood neighbor, Karen, and they spent all of their waking time together. They experienced a special childhood bond, which lasted until they were teenagers when Karen moved. This was understandably sad and difficult for Callie, but she'd learned what a good friendship is, which helped shape her future female relationships.

During Callie's teenage years, she experienced the challenges of being friends with other females, especially those who had to be the prettiest and most popular. Unfortunately, it's common in many adolescent female friendships to experience competition; and what seemed to matter most was who had the best hairstyle or wore the most stylish clothes. Status mattered, and so the focus was on popularity; however, Callie tried to maintain her friendships and feels she was successful.

Callie's friendships have meant a great deal to her, and she's learned to appreciate each one. She's especially grateful to the women who shared her challenges when she was a stay-at-home mom. As her children have grown, she has met other friends through common religious beliefs, and they continue to see each other and spend quality time together.

However, not every friendship is perfect, which Callie has become more aware of with age. She has struggled with one particular relationship which has lasted since childhood. Callie and Tracey went to the same school and had many mutual friends. But when Callie entered young adulthood and became a wife and mother, she and Tracey lost touch—not an uncommon occurrence.

Later, Callie worked at a school which Tracey's children attended. They rekindled their friendship and became closer than ever, given their shared history and positive memories. Tracey was soon hired at the same school, and so their time together increased, as did that of the two families. But there were bumps along the way when they disagreed. The two approached conflict differently; Callie wanted to talk about their issues, while Tracey preferred to avoid confrontation altogether. Coming to a resolution was impossible for Callie, and the frustration of these differing approaches increased the tension in the relationship.

There was a bigger bump that happened when Callie's marriage ended. Tracey felt the need to be brutally honest about what Callie should and should not do. Suddenly, Tracey became opinionated, and not in a good way. Callie was at a loss as to how to handle this change, especially because she felt she was being criticized and couldn't do anything right in Tracey's eyes. She also feels the shift was, in part, due to her becoming a divorcée, which Tracey considered horrible and negative. Callie not only began to feel judged, but also began to feel a power differential, which was uncomfortable and difficult to address with Tracey.

Callie still struggles with how to manage her feelings, and so she has created some distance with Tracey. Now she focuses on other important and meaningful friendships in her life, especially the ones in which she feels she can be open and honest. To her, these are vital qualities for lasting friendships.

ഔ Chapter Three ଔ

Dating Friends: Wait—what?

A wise woman once said to me, "Nicole, meeting and making friends is a lot like dating."

My response was, "What are you talking about?"

I imagined speed dating, and envisioned a female friend sitting in front me, which led me to think, *Wait— what? That's weird!* But thinking about the similarities between friendship and dating led me to think about the language used when speaking about each entity. For example, we have play-dates as children, and group dates or have group outings as we grow up. In college, some women participate in sorority rush, which is kind of like speed dating. You have a limited amount of time to get to know a group of women, and you need to assess whether or not you could be friends with them. If you're asked back, you have mini-dates. Culturally, we meet friends in very date-like ways; we get to know potential friends, just as we do potential romantic partners.

As I think more about my friendships, I'm amazed by how spot-on this woman is and how much effort we put into getting to know a potential friend. It's exhausting, yet can be very rewarding. Think about a good friend of yours. How did you meet? Do you remember how you exchanged contact information? Who initiated plans to hang out? After the first meeting, did one or both of you communicate to say, "That was fun!" or make a positive statement and express interest in meeting again?

It sounds a lot like dating, and we do this on a daily basis with potential friends. When we meet someone, we've made up our minds regarding whether or not we like them in about thirty seconds—very similar to meeting a potential romantic partner. We do this in many of our relationships, and then decide if we want to continue seeing a particular person.

We then go through the mating process. What are her likes and dislikes? What are her hobbies? Where did she go to school? After that test has been passed, we ask ourselves whether or not she is worth investing in, just as we would about a potential romantic partner. Why? Because as we mature, we may need this friend to be there for us in a way that was different than when we were ten years old. Instead of calling up a friend because Mom is being unfair, we may need to call this friend after we get a promotion or get fired and hope that she will be there for us.

If she becomes a friend and we label her as such, the honeymoon period begins—and it's glorious! You get to know each other on a deeper level, sharing your own stories. The honeymoon phase is very important because, as in a romantic relationship, it sets the stage for the rest of the friendship.

But all good things must end—well, not end, but slow down—and the friendship becomes established. There may be a spat or two, but if the friendship is stable, it will last. However, the friendship may fizzle out due to other pressing needs or roles. Maybe you or the friend begin dating, so the friendship takes a backseat to the new relationship (let's not pretend we don't do this). The testing of a friendship will prove whether it will last. Occasionally, the answer will not be evident for some time; in other cases, the friendship is reconnected at a later time, and the whole process begins again.

Surviving Female Friendships: The Good, The Bad, and The Ugly
~ Nicole Zangara

When the friendship is established, you both enter into a routine— keeping in contact through phone calls, e-mails and texts, planning get-togethers, and such. It's amazing how quickly this occurs and how effortless it is. The person becomes a part of your life. You may introduce her to other friends and bring her into your social circle; you may plan a road trip or a vacation together. By this point, you've probably told your family members about this new friend, and they may then invite her to a holiday brunch.

This sounds a lot like dating because it is. You invest time and energy in the relationship; you let down your guard and share personal stories, and learn to trust this person. Focusing on getting to know each other's history is important—and the friendship becomes significant and meaningful. If it's a successful friendship, you become closer and at some point may consider each other best friends (BFFs). This process can take from a couple of months to a couple of years. Experiencing this process is amazing and can be very fulfilling.

When you're dating, you're trying out a relationship; similarly, when you're getting to know a friend, you're assessing whether the friendship is worthwhile. The key question at this phase is whether the person and relationship is worth the effort when you don't know the outcome. At this time, the answer is usually yes; there's a reason you've became friends and shared experiences with this person.

However, as women get older, we become pickier about whom we choose to be our friends. We may not want to make the necessary investments if the relationship doesn't seem potentially worthwhile or feasible. If we've had friendships that ended badly, we may not be as open to meeting new friends and letting them into our lives. We use our past experiences as a compass for future ones—which is not always a good thing if we've been burned before. Also, as we become busier and have more responsibilities, we choose more carefully who we want in our corner. This can be very rewarding. Just as with a romantic partner to whom we commit for life, we hope that friendships will continue for the long term. We keep dating our friends until we figure out which are keepers and which are not.

This process of dating friends can be exhausting, but the benefits outweigh the costs when you hit the jackpot and meet someone who becomes one of your best friends. It's difficult to find "the one," and so this journey may not be easy; sometimes it feels like you're in the movie *Groundhog Day* and you're reliving the same moments with different people. However, it's important to continue putting yourself out there and to open yourself up to new adventures. Maybe this sounds silly, but I believe we have friendship soulmates, and it takes a while to find them. Some of you have found them already, and I raise my glass to you; others are still waiting for those good friends to come along. It's no easy feat; however, when you do meet that friendship soulmate, you'll know—and that feeling can't be explained in words.

Bethany: A Woman in Her 20s

Bethany's story is common among women. Her best friend from childhood, Hannah, gets engaged and Bethany is asked to be the maid of honor. This situation occurs in many female friendships, right? Not quite. Read on.

Bethany and Hannah's friendship spans more than ten years, and was one that Bethany thought would last a lifetime. As young girls, they played dress-up and talked about their wedding days; they shared their hopes and dreams for a common future.

Therefore, when Hannah asked Bethany to be her maid of honor, Bethany was thrilled. She gladly shared Hannah's happiness and was excited to do all the things expected of a maid of honor—dress-shopping, planning the bridal shower, and participating in all that goes along with a wedding. However, Bethany was in school, which made committing to every single event quite difficult. She shared her concerns with Hannah, who told her that it wasn't a problem. So, she didn't worry.

Bethany enjoyed the planning process; even though she lived in a different state, she was still able to be a significant part of it. She remembers going shopping for bridesmaid's dresses with Hannah and having a wonderful time. The experience was what the two had dreamed about as little girls. Bethany even became emotional when Hannah put on her wedding dress—because in that moment, everything became real. She felt happy, yet also sad, which is common when a best friend marries.

However, strange events began to occur. When it was time to plan the bridal shower, Bethany expressed concern about not being able to make it due to her obligations at school, as well as airfare costs. But the party was scheduled and would go on without Bethany, the maid of honor. She sent a gift and called Hannah, who told her that all went well, which made Bethany happy. She soon forgot that she had not been able to attend.

The bachelorette party was different. Bethany found that Hannah turned down everything she suggested, which made things difficult. She soon asked Hannah if something was wrong and was told there was not. Bethany figured it was the stress of the wedding and tried not to read more into the situation. Yet she felt something was off, but couldn't pinpoint exactly what it was.

Things went from bad to worse. With the wedding getting closer and things seeming strange in their friendship, she became worried and insecure. Additionally, with money still tight, she was unable to attend the bachelorette party, and felt awful about it. She called Hannah to see how the party went, and heard that it had been great. Bethany mentioned that many of the party's activities were her idea, and Hannah's attitude changed again. Now Bethany felt something was very, very wrong.

Just about a week before the big day, Hannah called Bethany and said she didn't want Bethany to give a planned speech at the wedding—the maid of honor's toast—which Bethany had been working on and looked forward to giving. Hannah's words stung. She also found out that one of Hannah's family members had been lying to Hannah about Bethany's involvement in the wedding planning process. Hannah's cousin lied to Hannah, taking all of the credit for the bachelorette party Bethany had planned. In addition, when Bethany needed to get some information for the wedding, she went into Hannah's e-mail (this was not abnormal for their friendship) and, to her dismay, found econversations in which she was made fun of and called awful names by Hannah and her cousin.

Bethany was terribly upset, angry, and humiliated by her best friend. She decided not to attend Hannah's wedding and sent her an e-mail telling her so; she even tried calling, but Hannah never answered her phone. Not attending the wedding was a difficult choice, but one she felt was right after finding out her best friend wasn't the person she thought.

Bethany still hasn't heard from Hannah, and becomes emotional when telling this story. Even though she still struggles with what happened, she feels she did the right thing by not attending the wedding and ending the friendship by no longer speaking to Hannah. But she has learned that she deserves respect from friends, and that people can change—and not always for the better.

ஓ Chapter Four ௸

Less Is More

Some of you identify yourselves as social butterflies; others prefer getting to know one or two people and tend to be more stay-at-home types. I'm going to make a large assumption based on my own social experiences and say it's not unusual for women to have fewer friends as we age. I'm sure some readers will disagree; however, I refer to those of us who have a handful of very close friends, and find satisfaction in these friendships.

In college, we tend to have many friends because we're around people of our own age all the time, and develop friendships through classes, study groups, and events. As we enter graduate school and/or full-time work, we become more focused on our independence and individuality. Thus, it's not unlikely that we want to spend the little free time we have with those we care about and feel

41

connected to—which is usually a select group of friends. Because we become more selective with our free time and want to be able to de-stress and have a good time during it, we focus on those friends who make us feel good.

When in graduate school, I learned that I was content having a few close friends and felt I was able to devote adequate time and energy to those friendships. I felt a deep connection with them and, even though it was not the usual college social experience, it provided what I needed. As I near thirty, I feel even more strongly that I need only a few good, close friends. It is these friends I confide in, and with whom I feel I can be myself. It's quality, not quantity.

Looking back, I realize that I've usually had a couple of close friends at a time because I felt satisfied with these few friendships and could focus on them. I've experienced all the phases of friendship I've described, which sometimes led to a close friendship and other times to just a really good conversation on a Saturday night. Sometimes I hung out regularly with a friend for a couple of months, but then she or I got busy, and that friendship receded while another picked up. Or maybe she started dating, got engaged, and became busy planning her wedding, and the focus shifted from the friendship to her new life with her husband.

Surviving Female Friendships: The Good, The Bad, and The Ugly
~ Nicole Zangara

As we grow older our focus changes, and so our friendships may suffer as we spend more time with partners, work, and/or children. I'm not minimizing the importance of friendships; however, it would be misleading to say that women who are in relationships and/or married don't shift their focus to that part of their life. This is a normal life progression. Being single allows more time for meeting potential romantic partners and making new friends.

It also becomes overwhelming to keep track of many friends when it's challenging enough to keep track of our own busy schedules and lives. Have you ever been in a room with three or four women? We like to talk, and because we're detail oriented, a story turns into an autobiography and we end up sharing more information than we needed to. But there can be pleasure and satisfaction in smaller gatherings with close friends because we're able to connect on a deeper level. This is why females have sleepovers, talk on the phone for hours, and spend entire days shopping together. In general, men don't engage in such activities. Females enjoy the company of their women friends and enjoy experiencing activities together, which can then be discussed, reflected upon, and retold.

It is these experiences that bond friends. When two or three women spend a lot of time together, they create intimate and powerful connections; this is more difficult to do in a group setting. Being able to give time and attention are vital to a friendship because you implicitly say, "You are meaningful to me and I want you to know that." It's also easier to develop a friendship when there's less distraction. When you're able to enjoy a friend's company, you provide the time and space to share and grow together.

On the other hand, some of you are comfortable with having a large number of friends. When I think back to my college experiences, a few women come to my mind who seemed to have a ridiculous number of friends; and they were always doing something with someone different. I have a hard time understanding how that works and how you juggle these friendships. Maybe I lack a multi-tasking gene—I find it difficult to keep track of everyone's schedules, including my own.

My hypothesis is that such women are more focused on the social aspect and the idea of spending time together, as well as sharing an activity; this is similar to action-driven male friendships. Perhaps some of you prefer getting a manicure with a friend rather than getting one by yourself, as you enjoy the company along with the activity instead of the emotional aspect of the interaction.

Surviving Female Friendships: The Good, The Bad, and The Ugly
~ Nicole Zangara

Part of me wonders if such friendships are deep, or if acquaintances and general connections generate a feeling of comfort. Another factor may be my need for meaningful connection and, therefore, only being open to having a few close friends for that to happen. In addition, it depends on your definition of "friend." For me, it's someone who's more than an acquaintance and to whom I feel close. For others, a friend may be someone you have fun with, not necessarily someone you count on or have any great attachment to. I think it comes down to personal preference, your personality, and how you define a friendship. Kudos to those of you who are social butterflies and feel secure in your friendships.

Esther, who is in her thirties, believes that as one grows older, it becomes almost a necessity to have a smaller group of friends. She's busy with her many roles; wife, daughter, sister, aunt, and artist, so she doesn't have the time to invest in a large group of friends. She feels lucky because she has two best friends, which is something Esther has not always experienced. She also has friends she sees every now and then and, while she enjoys the time she spends with them, she isn't looking for anything more at this point, as she's busy enough. Esther believes that when a woman is young and immature, she bases her self-worth on how many friends she has. This is common in college and high school, but later, a couple of close, rich friendships suffice.

Friendships are like a chocolate cake (I have a deep affection for chocolate); you can only hand out so many pieces until it's gone. This also applies to friendships—it's impossible to be available and connected to more than a couple of friends at one time. There are people who can do this, but I believe it comes more easily to men than women. Females invest in their friendships and want to be heard and validated by close friends, as is true of Esther—and me. When I'm on the phone with a friend, and she's listening, it can be incredibly helpful; if we add another caller, I have a more difficult time. Maybe my tolerance has decreased with age; I'm not able to handle as much drama and chaos, but I enjoy knowing I have a few close friends to whom I can reach out regularly and feel a sense of connection. It comes down to who you are and who you need or want in your life. Plus, the fewer people there are, the more chocolate cake left for me!

Jenny: A Woman in Her 30s

Jenny's story takes place in two locations. She was born and raised in North Carolina, but moved to New York when she was in her early twenties. At that time, she was in a committed relationship and busy with her job, and didn't make an effort to develop her own female friends. Instead, she spent most of her time with her boyfriend and his friends and partners, which worked for her. However, when Jenny and her boyfriend broke up a few years later, she was at a loss as to how to make her own friends and create her own life.

Because she found it difficult to make female friends, Jenny made the decision to move to a younger, hipper part of the city, hoping to meet new people. She also set a goal to get out more by attending happy hours with coworkers and going out on the weekends. Jenny got lucky—she started hanging out with the same people and going to the same hangouts, and she ultimately accomplished her goal. Even though she admits it wasn't easy, she feels it benefitted her because she became more confident and outgoing, and she met some very interesting women. These friendships became meaningful to Jenny.

After getting in a routine of spending time with friends, Jenny met her future husband James, who lived in North Carolina. It was a long-distance relationship, so in the beginning, it was easy to keep up with friends and spend one or two weekends a month with James. Her friends were happy for her, but knew that, at some point, she would have to make a decision, one that would most likely result in her moving back to North Carolina. In the meantime, she and James shared the burden of traveling to see each other.

As the relationship became serious, Jenny began to spend less time with her friends—not uncommon when women enter committed relationships. However, she still spent time with her friends when she was able to, which she enjoyed.

As time passed, some of Jenny's friends became involved in their own relationships; others were upset that her situation would result in marriage and her moving back to North Carolina. She found some of her single friends struggling with their own issues, as well as a pending loss and feelings of abandonment. It's often a struggle to find a healthy balance between friends and romantic partners.

Jenny did marry James and moved back to North Carolina. She looks back on this experience as one that many women share. She is grateful for her friends and the time she spent in New York City, and understands and appreciates more than ever the importance of balancing her friends and her marriage.

ಬ Chapter Five ಜ

Great Expectations

I have a love/hate relationship with the word "expectations"; it seems to have a negative connotation due to what we think about when the word comes to mind. When you're in school and the teacher describes her expectations for the assignment, you know what needs to be done to get an A in the class. When your mother says, "I expect you will be at dinner tonight," it gives you the sense that there's little to no room for discussion. In addition, the word can be associated with rules, which can be tricky to manage if you feel your friendship is rigid. For these reasons, when we or our friends have expectations, they're not always welcomed with open arms.

The word is a powerful tool in friendships; it's stating preferences in a strong manner. We all have expectations, large or small, good or bad, and we have them about friendships as well as other things. I've learned that I have high self-expectations about personal growth and learning. I could blame my parents for these, but that wouldn't be totally accurate, as I've always pushed myself. I don't apologize for these expectations because I believe they helped me to achieve. I had expectations that I would do well in school, go to college, and then get my Master of Social Work. Expectations not only keep us going, but they also keep us in check when we fail and realize our expectations may have been too high. That's what makes us human; we succeed and fail, yet we still come out okay... or at least we hope so.

Regarding my expectations for friendships, I've had to re-examine and question them. Is it fair to have expectations for our friends? Why or why not? Depending on your view of expectations, you may not see them as negative, but your friend may. It depends on your experience with expectations, if you have them, and to what extent they impact your friendships. The key is defining the expectation and making it clear to the friend. For example, if I loan you twenty-five dollars, I hope that someday, if I'm in need of twenty-five dollars, you'll loan me the money. Is that an expectation or an appropriate give-and-take? I find that many people struggle with this idea and I think it affects many friendships. I've heard friends say that they hate owing people money so they avoid the situation altogether. Expectations are easily misunderstood because everyone defines them differently for themselves and for others.

Money is worth discussing when attempting to figure out expectations for friends because it's an area that's always difficult to navigate in friendships. In today's economy, women who are still in school and/or starting their careers are likely paying off student loans and don't have much ready cash. It can be awkward to discuss money when there are feelings of shame and embarrassment regarding one's salary, debt, or loans.

Expectations can arise from money matters without us even realizing it and can become a source of resentment. For example, I know many women who have given their best friend money to help her out during a financially hard time. Once there is an exchange of money, some of you may find it difficult not to want that money back or feel there is an uneven dynamic in the friendship. Telling your friend, "I got this. Don't worry," is nice, but at some point there needs to be reciprocation. If there isn't, the friendship could become a way for the friend to be pampered, instead of engaging in a healthy friendship.

Surviving Female Friendships: The Good, The Bad, and The Ugly
~ Nicole Zangara

Unless you live in a mansion on a private island, money is a touchy subject. It's especially challenging when there's an expectation that you'll loan money or cover a bar tab without the other person reciprocating. It's safe to assume that we all have friends who do this and you can probably name a few right now. You probably even have names for them, like moochers, takers, or users. The idea of friendship and dating applies here because friends may think it's okay to do this since you usually have cash. Plus, if you haven't said anything, why would there be a problem? News alert: this is not okay! Many people can be taken advantage of in such situations.

Frankly, I'm quite bothered by this situation. People hesitate to speak up and be assertive because money is so tricky to discuss. I have very little patience for friends who never seem to have cash to pay for even part of an outing; I view that as a feeling of entitlement and a lack of manners. I'm not saying that you need to keep score on each meal or outing, but there needs to be an acknowledgement of fairness. It might be entertaining to carry a piece of paper and tally up every expense and who pays for it, but you may lose friends quickly that way.

In defining my expectations in relationships, I see loyalty and consideration as components that factor into expectations; however, I acknowledge that you may have a different outlook. I'm a perfectionist, so my expectations can get in the way of my friendships. I put my heart and soul into things, and if I feel what I'm putting into a friendship is not being returned, I feel let down.

When I enter into a friendship, I do so wholeheartedly; I can't do it half-heartedly, because I don't understand what the point would be. It's possible that this is partly due to my all-or-nothing mentality. If I view you as my friend, I care about you and want you to know that. I like to reach out by sending "thinking of you" texts or e-mails, or by calling. That's how I work, and I understand that not everyone is like that. But it's hard for me when I feel I'm not getting the same back. However, I've now learned that I can't be all-or-nothing, and so I try to see everything in-between. A friend once assured me that it's not bad to have expectations; I just have to understand that not everyone can meet them. I attempt to keep my expectations in check by knowing that friends can only give what they're capable of giving, which is true of me as well. Sometimes we feel slighted, or as if we're carrying the load. Finding balance is not easy; it requires special care and thought, as it differs and may change with each friendship.

Surviving Female Friendships: The Good, The Bad, and The Ugly
~ Nicole Zangara

We have different expectations for our friends than we do for our parents or our siblings. If we feel we're being let down by a friend, it's more difficult to address those feelings than if we feel let down by a family member. For example, if I'm mad at my mother/father/sibling, I call her/him up and yell. But I wouldn't do that with a friend; I try to be a little more mature. My family will not breakup with me, but a friend may. Some may disagree, but addressing this topic with friends can create a perception of being high maintenance or needy.

Being held back by these fears leads to feelings of disappointment and anger; these feelings prevent the friendship from growing, and each friend understanding the expectations of the other. You don't hear friends saying to each other, "Now listen, I expect X, Y, and Z from you. Do you agree?" We are not that explicit. But think what it would be like if we were more open with our expectations. Would it be such a bad thing? As we get older and become more secure in ourselves, we also know what we do and don't want. And, hopefully, we become more self-confident and able to assert our opinions and feelings. Why does that sometimes seem impossible to do in a friendship?

I believe it's because we're afraid of losing our friends as we age. There is a sense of commitment and investment in our friendships that increases as we mature, so the idea of losing a good friend can be scary. We want to hold on to these friendships, especially if we've known the person for more than five years; if the friendship has lasted since elementary school, there's a level of connection that's hard to negate.

I recently experienced conflict in one of my friendships and, because the relationship had spanned about eight years, neither of us wanted to walk away. So we instead agreed that there was work to be done, but that the friendship was not over. Both of us wanted to hold on because of our history. It's hard to say what the outcome would have been if the friendship were new or not as deep.

Friends provide stability and comfort when we most need it, and thinking that we may lose that anchor is frightening. It's as if we're losing a part of our identity and history. So rather than share our expectations up front, we begin the friendship holding back our thoughts and feelings because we don't want to seem too demanding or direct. Why, you ask? Because we all know that stereotypical female who is high maintenance and all about getting her needs met now. We fear that if we come across as too aggressive or strong, we'll scare people off. While that may be true if you're giving orders left and right, that's probably your fears talking—and they're not all that rational. As discussed in the first chapter, women who are direct are perceived as She Devils; so I believe that some of you feel that if you share your expectations, that's how friends may view you.

I challenge you to face those fears and to be more honest with yourself, as well as with your friends. Maybe you will find out that your expectations are shared, or that others have had similar experiences. And maybe you'll be seen as confident and secure in yourself, rather than being seen as demanding and aggressive. Women who know what they want and are not afraid to show it are usually successful—like Oprah, Hillary Clinton, and Betty Friedan, to name a few.

Another facet of expectations is their intricacy, especially regarding that friend (we all have one) who is unreliable. We know from the beginning that this person is not one who will follow through, and that she's a friend to have a good time with and be silly. We often learn which categories to put a friend in based on her verbal and non-verbal behavior. We all have friends we can call up and talk to for hours, and we all have friends who are better for going out and having a good time with. Over time, we begin to see which friend will show up, and which friend is always busy and impossible to reach. Sometimes, though, we're surprised when the latter comes through and, for the time being, our expectations change. That is the humorous, yet frustrating part of friendships—we're constantly shifting and adjusting to new levels of expectations, depending on where we and our friends are emotionally and mentally.

Nancy: A Woman in Her 60s

Nancy's expectations have changed over the years. Her friendships are important and mean a great deal to her. She has found that many of her relationships change constantly, yet each one is special and impacts her life positively. Some of Nancy's friendships are stronger than others, yet each one has given her something to appreciate.

Through her many experiences, Nancy has learned that when she's able to meet a friend "where the friend is at that time" and is aware of what the friend's expectations of her are, the result is a satisfying friendship. She has come to understand that she values the woman's qualities, character, and ability to resolve conflict, as well as her ability to reciprocate appreciation and respect. She also believes that when friends are open to sharing themselves with each other, it brings them closer and allows for greater understanding.

Nancy enjoys this sense of connection and getting to know a friend in ways that acquaintances do not share.

However, it took Nancy a long time to have such a patient outlook on expectations. When she was younger, she didn't understand that one person can't meet all our friendship needs, or that relationships go through ups and downs. Looking back, Nancy sees that she expected much from others and gave little, and she anticipated that her friends would know her and always understand her thoughts and feelings. When a friend wasn't available, she reacted by becoming judgmental and felt the emotions that come with disappointment. She understands how easy it is to be let down by friends because she has experienced these feelings.

Now older and wiser, Nancy is able to understand that not all of her friends can meet all of her needs. She is also able to see that a friend's bad mood or unreturned phone call may not be about her, but rather about what the friend is going through at a given time. She tries to understand what's going on with her friends, which has helped to lower her expectations. Nancy has found that, having made these changes in her expectations, she is happier and more satisfied in her friendships, and experiences less chaos and drama.

Surviving Female Friendships: The Good, The Bad, and The Ugly
~ Nicole Zangara

Nancy's story helps women like me who struggle with expectations; it helps to take a step back from a friendship and be realistic about what someone is capable of giving, as well as what may be going on in her life.

Sometimes it's best to simply enjoy your friends and focus on each person's positive qualities rather than focusing on what she does or doesn't do. It's helpful to be grateful for the friends who are in our lives now, instead of those who are distant, out of reach, or not meeting our needs. Friends can only give what they are capable of at that moment in time, and the same goes for us; at some point, we will fail each other and the friendship. It's vital to remember this. I'm fairly certain that I've let down many of my friends; it is inevitable. The tricky part is discussing these situations and learning from them.

Expectations are part of any friendship, whether we admit it or not. We have expectations that keep the foundation of the friendship stable. We expect a friend to show up when we schedule a dinner or coffee date; that when she says she will call you after work, she will. However, life is not perfect, and we make mistakes, we forget, and ultimately fail our friends. The solution is to discuss these occurrences and to expect the unexpected.

At the end of the day, the only person you can rely on is yourself. Yes, our friends can provide support and comfort, but thinking that one friend can meet all our needs is illogical. How would you feel if a friend looked to you to meet all of her needs? You'd probably run for the nearest exit.

It's healthy and appropriate to have expectations in your friendships; however, it's about having ones that don't exceed the friend's capabilities. Just like in Nancy's story, it's helpful to take a step back, re-evaluate your expectations, and appreciate each friend for who she is, not who you want her to be. We have no control over that.

Lacy: A Woman in Her 20s

Lacy is a grounded, twenty-something woman who has her act together. When she shared her story with me, I was taken aback by the soap-opera qualities that seemed at odds with her sweet nature. Keep this in mind as you continue.

Lacy explains that she's always struggled with her female friendships. From girlhood to early adulthood, she thought these relationships were challenging and finding good friends was impossible. When she got to college, however, Lacy made some lasting friendships, for which she is thankful. But she did have a painful post-college experience with a female friend.

Lacy started spending time with a guy named Adam, which led to them becoming more than friends and spending even more time together. Lacy says that she and Adam were technically not a couple, as they didn't label their relationship as boyfriend/girlfriend. However, everyone who knew them knew they were sleeping together and the relationship had gone beyond friendship territory. This had been going on for over a year, so it wasn't a fling or a one night stand. They weren't exclusive; but Lacy was, due to her beliefs and morals. To her, sex meant something. However, Adam was not like Lacy; he was a player, and he'd had many prior romantic relationships, while Lacy had only had a few.

When Lacy's friend, Janet, entered the picture, things got messy. The two women met through Adam, which was a positive thing in the beginning. Janet was married, and had a larger-than-life ring to prove it. Lacy and Janet spent time together, enjoying artsy activities and spending time with Adam. Lacy says Janet's husband was kind of a jerk, which is Lacy's polite way of saying he was much worse than that.

Lacy also says that Janet's husband tended to overreact, so she would cover for her friend. She cared for

Janet and wanted to help her in any way she could. There was one particular instance when Janet went to hang out with Lacy; Janet's husband called Lacy to make sure his wife was telling the truth. After that time, even if Janet wasn't with Lacy, she would cover for her by telling Janet's husband that she was with her. Looking back, Lacy realizes that this wasn't the best decision, but she's the first to admit that she's not always made the best decisions when it comes to her friends. And she's still learning.

Throughout the friendship, Lacy shared intimate details with Janet about her relationship with Adam, and Janet shared her marital woes. It was a friendship that had no bounds. Lacy has since realized how dangerous it can be to share such personal thoughts and feelings; at the time, however, the two became the best of friends and continued to share secrets. They also spent a lot of time with Adam.

Looking back, Lacy realizes that she should've known what was really going on, but she didn't; she was just enjoying her friendship with Janet and her romantic relationship with Adam. Things seemed to be going fine. When other people expressed their concerns regarding Janet and Adam, Lacy shrugged it off. She felt strongly that nothing was happening because Janet was married and she considered her to be her best friend. It was impossible that Janet would do anything to hurt her, right? Wrong.

When the rose-colored glasses came off, Lacy felt as though she'd been hit by a truck. She called Janet to ask for the truth and to prove the naysayers wrong. Janet affirmed the truth, and Lacy was in shock. Not only had Lacy been with Adam just a few weeks before, but Janet defended her actions; she even made comments about how this has nothing to do with Lacy. Wow. She also brought up personal things Lacy had shared about an innocent crush she had on another guy, as well as saying that Lacy and Adam weren't even dating, which only poured salt into the deep, open wounds.

Lacy and Janet's relationship ended, and Lacy has no intention to resurrect it. She feels anger, resentment and, above all, pain. She couldn't believe that someone who was supposed to be her best friend would have a relationship with the guy she was seeing. It took her a lot of time to get over it. To this day, she still cannot believe what happened, and is stunned that Janet didn't respect her enough to talk with her about what she was doing with Adam.

Lacy feels she learned a lot about people through this experience, and told me sometimes two people have such different ways of thinking and doing things that they can't be friends; differences can overcome a friendship. Lacy believes it was her morals that caused her to end her relationship with Janet.

After this happened, Lacy tried her best to remain friends with their group; but it proved impossible. Every interaction with Janet was awkward, and remaining friends with Adam was even more difficult due to his obvious alliance with Janet. When Lacy heard about the comments and rude remarks Janet was making behind her back, she felt undermined, yet realized that's the type of person Janet is. Adam, however, saw what he wanted and stuck up for Janet. Now Lacy understands that the two deserve each other.

This experience has also led Lacy to wonder about her friends and those who know her for who she is; she has had to rethink many of her relationships, and looks more carefully at the people around her. She told me that, to her, driving a friend to the airport and/or picking her up is what makes a good friend great. I found that interesting because I always struggle with whom to ask, as it can be such an inconvenience. For Lacy, a good friend will say yes, and goes the extra mile. Sometimes it's the little things friends say or do that mean the world to us.

Lacy strongly believes that you should always take the high road and not do or say things you'll regret. As in the situation with Janet, there were times when she could've bad-mouthed Janet, but that's not the type of person Lacy is. Moreover, she believes that if two people can approach a conflict as mature adults, the likelihood of the friendship surviving is fairly good. However, if there are words and moments that can't be taken back, the likelihood is not so good. It comes down to treating others with respect; Lacy believes that this is the one thing she can control, so she continues to do her best.

℘ Chapter Six ☙

Honesty: Is It The Best Policy?

I struggle with this topic because I'm an honest person. Also, my parents taught me to be honest, so I can justifiably blame them for this annoying trait. I'd rather tell someone what I think and feel than sugarcoat my opinion or lie—but it's not that easy in female friendships. So when a good friend asks about her appearance, weight, partner, and/or new pair of shoes, I wish there were a pause button I could press to have time to think about my answer. I would need about three minutes to give an appropriate and genuine answer. "Yes, Ellen, your partner is very nice." Or, "Ellen, those shoes are definitely your style!" Maybe these answers seem like cop-outs, but I believe that sometimes honesty does not help a friendship.

One could argue that if you've been friends with a woman for ten years rather than one month, your answer may be different. I agree. If you're just getting to know a person, you may say something that unintentionally hurts her feelings. Also, an unintended meaning can be read into an e-mail or text, which could also land you in trouble. An established friendship may provide a GPS system to navigate such areas, so it's more likely you'll know what to say and how to say it. Moreover, an established friendship has most likely already allowed a discussion of those topics that are off the table. In longtime friendships, it's highly safe to assume that you've appropriately dealt with conflict, so a disagreement or difference of opinion is not a big deal. In new friendships, conflict can be daunting because managing it can influence the outcome of the friendship.

There is a fine line in learning how to be honest with a friend, and you may need to have a conversation about it. It doesn't have to be super-serious, but it may be helpful to have a discussion about topics that are sensitive for each party. We don't always know what and how honest comments will affect the other person, because they may evoke our vulnerabilities and insecurities. When we're honest about our feelings, it's possible that we're opening ourselves up to judgment, criticism, or dismissive comments; and no one wants to feel judged for how they feel or think. That's why it's important to discuss your feelings as they come up in different situations and conversations.

For example, a friend and I were texting each other. I had a negative reaction to something she wrote—I took offense to a comment she made about me. I texted back and straightforwardly let her know how I felt. After some time passed, I wasn't sure if I'd overreacted, so I texted again, apologizing. She texted back and told me not to apologize for my feelings.

I felt good that I could be honest and wasn't dismissed for sharing my honest thoughts. Her validation made me feel she was receptive and open to my feelings, and so I was glad I could be honest with her. Of course, this episode could have turned out much differently if she reacted negatively. Similarly, if I hadn't addressed my feelings then, this situation very well could've happened again and resulted in an overreaction due to unresolved feelings.

In friendships, we too often let things go because we fear how the person will respond. Many women wait until it's too late to be honest, and then all the pent-up frustration pours forth, sometimes in a most untactful way. We fear that we'll be seen as too picky or sensitive, which takes us back to expectations and how they influence friendships. However, if you don't speak up when a friend makes a comment that rubs you the wrong way, there may be a problem if she makes the remark again. You may "let her have it" when she didn't know her statement was bothering you in the first place.

No matter the type of friendship, it's important to be truthful. Honesty is something we're taught at a young age, and it's a valued trait. Sure, we all throw out the occasional white lie or fib; but staying true to the friendship by not being afraid to be honest will only make the relationship stronger.

Delivery can be critical—how you present your honest thoughts and feelings. Delivery can be everything. Remember the adage, *It's not what you say, it's how you say it*. Telling someone how you feel is extremely difficult, so choose your words wisely. Be mindful about what you say and how you say it, and be open to the feedback. If you don't do these things, it may lead to conflict.

So the question remains: is honesty the best policy? I'm going to leave the answer up to you, as it will differ with each friend. If the discussion is about your thoughts and feelings regarding the friendship, I encourage you to be honest. If the discussion is about your friend's boyfriend, that may be an explosion waiting to happen. Use your judgment, yet pay attention to your feelings and how they may be impacting the friendship. Don't be afraid to express them.

❧ Chapter Seven ☙

Conflict: Can't We Just Make Up?

I'm not going to make conflict sound pretty. Conflict sucks. It's difficult to sit with another person hashing out your differences. If the friendship is solid and worth saving, conflict—although tough—can strengthen the bond between friends. It's not easy to tell a friend that you feel hurt, or to hear that you hurt someone else. And it can be even harder to know how to validate her feelings when you may feel you didn't wrong her in the first place.

I become defensive easily. (I'm sure everyone who knows me is probably nodding emphatically and glad to read that I'm admitting my faults.) My go-to defense mechanism is, well, defensiveness; so when conflict rears its ugly head, that's how I react. In situations where I'm not as confident, I shut down. So there it is.

Neither of these maneuvers help to resolve conflict. Defensiveness and shutting down only deepen conflict's abyss. Think for a second about how you approach conflict. Do you put on your shields and protective gear, or do you sit with your arms and legs crossed? Remember, non-verbal behavior can be just as noticeable and effective as verbal behavior.

It's extremely important to be aware of the ways in which people approach conflict, because it will happen in your friendship. If you've never had a disagreement with a friend, you are lying and/or in denial. The first fight or difference of opinion in a friendship can be frightening if you're not well versed in how women approach conflict. So here I am, ready to help as best I can.

Each individual is unique, with her own way of communicating her thoughts and feelings. So when something happens in the friendship that causes tension or stress, each woman will manage it differently. Some women become confrontational; perhaps that was how they were taught to resolve conflict. They may call you the B-word and tell you to go screw yourself, and then will want to grab a drink after work the next day. They've said their piece and are over it and ready to move on, while you may still be in shock that they've used so many curse words in one breath.

71

Other women will pull back, giving themselves time to think about what they will say or do; yet others become extremely emotional. Added to the mix is the fact that some women may want to talk and sort things out then and there, while others refuse to take any of the responsibility, and then put the blame on you.

And the kicker to all of this is that we may change the way we communicate depending on the way the other communicates. Lovely, right? If I'm in conflict with a friend and she starts to yell at me, I'll probably shut down. However, if I'm in conflict with a friend and she starts to cry, I'll probably feel bad and say I'm sorry right away while handing her a box of tissues. It depends on both people's styles, but be careful. They vary among friends, so we may need to bring a variety of armor and weapons to the battlefield.

We all have different ways in which we communicate and resolve conflict, and our style may clash with the other person's. This can make it challenging to figure out which style, among those noted above or others, your friend has after your first fight. It's sometimes unclear as to where the friendship stands and how to get back to normal. "Are we okay?" may be asked, and replies can range from "Yeah, of course!" to "No, I need some space." The first fight and how it is or isn't resolved can impact the rest of the friendship. Think back to your first fight with your closest friend. How did you resolve the fight? How did each of you approach the conflict? How did it feel to be in conflict? Did it take time to get back to normal?

I believe there is an art of conflict; I just haven't figured it out yet. Part of it is hearing what the other person says, and then acknowledging and validating her feelings. You may not agree, but would you rather hear your friend say, "I'm sorry you feel hurt" versus "Well, I didn't do anything wrong." It's not easy to look at the situation and ask yourself, *How would I feel if I were in her shoes? Would I be upset?* Sometimes you have to agree to disagree and try to move past the conflict because there may be no resolution.

Many of us pretend there's no conflict in our friendships, but it's there, and we need to find better ways to handle it. Why do we avoid conflict? Because we're not taught how to manage it appropriately (unless you're becoming a trained peer mediator or you major in conflict resolution) and it's not openly discussed. Learning how to manage conflict is not something one can prepare for because it can be unpredictable and may not have the outcome you hoped. Haven't you heard a friend talk about a situation she's in with another friend, discuss her game plan,

73

then tell you the next day that it didn't go at all the way she thought? You can prepare as much as possible, but it comes down to how you handle the conflict in the moment—what you say and do, not what you will say and do. It's how you react that has the biggest impact, not how well you memorized what you were going to say.

If you can understand that conflict comes in many forms and disguises, then you may be able to see that conflict is all around us, and how easily people sweep it under the carpet. The next time you're at your workplace or the grocery store, pay attention to people's exchanges and look for verbal and non-verbal behavior. The teenager who gives her parent an eye roll or answers a question defensively; the husband who asks his wife if she really needs another pair of shoes; the woman who tells her friend that she's mad at her for telling another friend a secret. Some of us are aggressive in conflict and directly can tell our friend how we're feeling; others are passive-aggressive and too afraid to even disagree with anything our friend says or does. Conflict is everywhere, and one valuable thing to learn is that, in friendships, it's okay to have a different opinion and to feel comfortable stating it.

Another reason we avoid conflict is because we don't want to think that someone disagrees with us or that we did something wrong. Acknowledging our wrongdoings is admitting failure—and no one likes to do that. We don't want to think we caused someone pain or discomfort. Additionally, apologizing is not easy, and if it's seen as forced or fake, it causes more conflict. Have you experienced an apology which felt as though the person were pulling her own teeth? It's not pleasant, and you're left feeling angrier. It takes a lot of courage to recognize that we made a mistake, and even more to understand and accept that we need to own those mistakes.

Attempting resolution is usually difficult, and questions often remain. Where do we go from here? Will things get back to normal? Will I/she make the same mistake again? Is it a bad sign that there's conflict in the friendship? Of course, friends can move past conflict, but it requires finding a healthy balance of conflict in a friendship. Two people, no matter how similar, will not agree on everything. Have you ever gone shopping with a friend? Enough said.

In addition, feelings can get hurt when there's conflict, and we have to be careful how we address those feelings. Again, women tend to be more emotional than men, and so they're frequently more sensitive to things their friends say or do. It's not easy to face a friend when you feel hurt, or when she tells you how she really feels about your boyfriend. We may not admit it, but we care about how our friends think and feel about us, so when there's conflict, it can create doubt in the foundation of the friendship. There needs to be awareness that words impact our feelings and, because of our deep connections to our friends, can do greater damage.

Trying to work through conflict is important, and it can save a friendship; inadequately addressed conflict can unnecessarily end a relationship. There's no guarantee that conflict will be completely resolved; but it's important that both people be open and honest, and discuss their feelings instead of avoiding them. There's usually no need to speak up about each incident; choose your battles carefully, and perhaps limit them to things that irritate you. For example, if you always initiate get-togethers or communication by calling or texting, it would be appropriate to bring that up with a friend in a non-judgmental way. For instance, it could go like this; "Hey Maggie, I really enjoy hanging out and talking with you, yet I've noticed that I'm the one who usually initiates things. Maybe I'm reading too much into this, but would it be okay if you called me, too? I would love to hear from you." Or perhaps you always drive when you go out, and feel the other person should offer, or at least offer to pay the valet fee. "Hey Maggie, I feel as if almost every time we hang out, I drive and end up paying the valet fee. While I really enjoy spending time with you, what do you think about splitting or maybe alternating these fees and/or who drives?" These are small issues, but can become huge if not appropriately addressed. Sometimes all it takes is a casual comment.

Conflict is uncomfortable. Mind you, some people think conflict is fun and they enjoy confronting others—but they are in a unique category. To most people, conflict is overwhelming and, if you're not used to it, will seem like a foreign language. My hope is that as people become more aware of their "hot buttons" or are able to see problems in their friendships, they'll become more comfortable discussing these issues. There's no right or wrong way, as long as both parties come to the conversation with an open mind and open heart. Wouldn't that be nice?

By this point, I hope you've noticed that fear in friendships is addressed here frequently, and how just about anything can trigger fear—from our expectations, to trying to be honest, to conflict. The next time you're unsure about a friendship, ask yourself if you're feeling fear. Then ask yourself what the fear is about. Are you afraid the friend will leave you? Yell at you? Tell you that you're being ridiculous? After you've gone through all the hypothetical answers, ask yourself again if your fear is talking. Be honest with yourself about what's going on with your feelings.

Sometimes we're our own worst enemies, creating our own barriers without even realizing it. We see a pool and think, "It looks too cold for a swim." So we dip a toe in, and soon come to realize the water is quite nice. We live our lives with many assumptions, which sometimes turn out not to be correct. And we can let fear paralyze us and take control of us, which doesn't help any friendship become stronger.

If we have experienced difficult or painful friendship breakups, we may be especially sensitive and bring that emotional baggage into our potential friendships. We all have baggage—some more than others—and instead of ignoring it, try to be aware of it and how it affects your friendships and your overall outlook. Whether it's expectations or attempting to be honest with your friend about conflict, understand that sometimes we simply have to take that leap of faith and jump in the water. We may be surprised by how good it feels to let the fear go.

Olivia's story is a great example of a situation in which there is conflict, attempts to be honest and make expectations clear, and how it all can go haywire when there's little or no communication.

Olivia: A Woman in Her 40s

Olivia's story is one of the classic bridezilla types—you know the book would be incomplete without at least one. Olivia met Kim through work and they became the best of friends. When women spend every day together and discover that they have a connection with each other, it often results in a lasting friendship—and that was the case here.

When Kim got engaged, she asked Olivia to be a bridesmaid. Under normal circumstances, one would be happy and excited about this role. After some time passed, however, Kim told Olivia that she didn't think she was doing her bridesmaid's duties well and was not providing her with enough support. Olivia was confused and didn't understand what Kim was talking about; she was also angry because she wasn't the maid of honor, who should've been carrying out the duties—not her.

Olivia soon found out that there was conflict between Kim and the real maid of honor, one of Kim's family members, which made her the de facto maid of honor, without the title. In retrospect, Olivia believes that Kim's anger was inappropriately directed at her, when it was clear that she and her real maid of honor had a lot to work through. However, she was at a loss as to how to address this with Kim. She tried her best to be supportive through the wedding, but never really understood what her role was. Sadly, due to this experience, their friendship never returned to normal, and they have yet to discuss what happened.

ఐ Chapter Eight ಆ

Complex Friendship Situations

$\mathcal{A}$s I become older, my friendships are changing, and I'm having a difficult time keeping up. It seems that people's lives are becoming more complicated, and so we're constantly learning new ways to adapt. There are a number of situations I've come across for which sadly, I have no answers, but believe need to be addressed. So the next time you experience a "Why me?" moment, please know that we all go through these often bizarre and unexplainable situations.

Situation 1: Engaged and/or Married Friends

Many of my friends are engaged and/or married, so the friendships have changed from, "I" to "we," and the "we" doesn't mean her and me. When we make plans to get together, these friends usually check with their spouses—or invite them, which makes me feel like a third wheel. I do have fun, but there's a feeling that something is missing, which is no one's fault. Having engaged and/or married friends is part of getting older and going through natural life stages. This process is an integral part of life. However, it can be challenging when you're the one still looking for Mr. or Ms. Right (depending on your sexual orientation), and some of your friends are already living that part.

Diane, a woman in her forties, shares her thoughts about being on the other side. She brings a fresh perspective because, being in a relationship, she struggles with single friends. There is one in particular, Tanya, who is having a very tough time with Diane's relationship status; every time they talk, Tanya focuses only on her single status. Diane understands and can appreciate Tanya's struggles, but at some point it becomes overwhelming. Now Diane feels like she's walking on eggshells every time they talk because she's afraid to discuss her future plans which usually involve her boyfriend. She feels as if she has to self-censor what she says which makes conversations difficult. She also worries that not sharing what's happening in her life is creating more distance in a friendship that used to be solid.

Diane now wonders what it was like for her married friends when she was the single one. Friends not being in the same place in life can be difficult even though Diane believes it shouldn't make or break a friendship. However, she acknowledges that it can be an arduous path to navigate. It has made Diane more aware of where her friends are in their lives, and she appreciates how a romantic relationship can impact friendships. This is somewhat new to her, since she was single for many years.

Diane's story makes it clear that one friend's relationship can make a friendship problematic for both parties. It also gives both the single and attached perspectives, which can be useful when you find yourself experiencing ill feelings toward your single or married friends. Remember that the changes impact everyone involved, and your friend may also feel she can't share things with you because you're not sharing the same experience. It unintentionally creates distance in the friendship—and it's hard not to notice the change. Of course, you're happy for a friend who has found her soulmate, but it can still be tough to manage the effect on the friendship. When you're the single one, it can bring up many emotions to see close friends moving on; jealousy, sadness, and even anger, to name a few. Of course, we're happy for our friends, but it wouldn't be accurate if I didn't discuss the other feelings we experience, especially those no one likes to talk about. Or, when you're the one in a relationship, it may be challenging to see single friends struggling with their own issues.

There are many ways in which we move on besides marriage; however, marriage is a major life event and it needs to be addressed. A friend marrying means that the friendship will certainly change (see the film *Bridesmaids*). Friends may need to discuss the foreseeable changes and how to manage the feelings that will come up on both sides. This will allow each person to be heard and validated, as well as provide the time and place for both of you to share your fears, both of which are critical to the friendship. Such a conversation may lay the groundwork for future significant life changes, which will not seem so tricky if that ground has already been covered.

Situation 2: No Response

Things are about to get a little more complicated, so settle in for this question. What about when a friend stops returning texts/e-mails/calls, and you don't understand why? Friendships go through changes as we get busy and need our space, but I have found that some friendships seem to drop off the face of the earth. These are the friendships that seemed so constant and so reliable—then, one day, they unexpectedly shift to an entirely different level. This type of situation tends to happen more as we age due to new and demanding life responsibilities and priorities. Maybe the friend started a new job and is extremely busy; perhaps she's going through something and isn't quite ready to call you and tell you about it. The complicated part is that we sometimes have absolutely no idea what happened and we may just have to wait for the storm to pass.

I will say that I tend to create my own version of what's happening—in part to keep myself entertained, but also as a way to try to understand the drastic change. Maybe she was abducted by aliens and doesn't have her cell phone, or maybe she has a secret lover and is afraid to tell her friends about him. Of course, these examples are ludicrous, but sometimes our minds wander because what is happening doesn't seem logical. The other way I handle such situations is to ask myself if I've done something wrong. Many women blame themselves or take a magnifying glass to every recent conversation and interaction. Put the magnifying glass down and step away. But the key question is this: why is it so hard to ask the person what's going on?

It's troublesome to stop hearing from a friend, and equally so to figure out how to handle the situation. Sometimes a phone call or e-mail asking if everything's okay is sufficient; however, there's a fine line between giving the person space and being intrusive. I have no answer as to why people stop responding. It's hard not to acknowledge what is going on and especially hard not to think something happened—or, worse, that you did something wrong. Sometimes you have to believe that the friendship is strong enough to bounce back or that the friend will come around when she is able or willing. This is a situation that I find incredibly difficult, especially if you consider the person a good friend.

Situation 3: Office Friendships

We often become close to female co-workers as we share a lot of time and experiences together. As these friendships develop, we may start to spend time together outside the office—maybe at a happy hour or driving to a conference. Many office friendships provide validation and support when we need it most, and can be extremely helpful with day-to-day stress. You know you can walk into your female friend's office and say, "I'm having the worst period EVER!" and feel as though she'll understand.

Female office friendships fill daily needs that other friendships may not. It's difficult to explain your day at work to a friend who has no idea what you're talking about or why it's so upsetting. So when we change jobs or move, female work friendships may dissolve because we no longer need that support. It's not a good or bad thing, but it does happen. The more time you spend with someone, the closer you will become; this is true of all friendships and relationships.

Emily, who is in her thirties, has noticed that as she gets older, she has many circles and networks of friends. These include her work friends, mommy friends, neighbors, and friends she's met through her husband. She notes that each network is independent and rarely mixes. She's learned that when one of these networks closes down—by leaving a job or using a different daycare provider—the friendships are difficult to maintain because the daily contact is lost. Starting new ventures begins the cycle again.

It's important to look at constant change as new opportunities, because it can be downright depressing if we're always yearning for the past and who was in it, rather than looking at those in front of us. Instead of focusing on how there's no longer as much communication with a friend, it may be helpful to appreciate how she was there for you during a critical time. Many of our friends demonstrate their friendship during times of crisis, so remembering that a work friend spent hours listening to you talk about your mean boss will remind you that she is/was a good friend. If there's a drastic change in communication, a check-in may be needed, and may help to reconnect you both in a different way.

Situation 4: Constant Transition Rollercoaster

Change is important to address because, as our situations change and we move from one life stage and event to another, the constant transitioning can be overwhelming. As we become older, we are in constant flux—and I'm not sure it ever slows down. Why is it that when we look back on our childhood it all seemed so much easier? We didn't have school loans, bills, crazy landlords, or stressful jobs. As adults, it's as if we're circus performers, juggling all our responsibilities and wearing many hats on any given day. Also, as we mature, we take on more responsibilities. Maybe we'd like to be a Toys-R-Us kid forever—but that's impossible. Instead, we're making important life decisions that require significant time and careful consideration. We're deciding how much money to put into a 401K, determining where we want to settle down, buying our first home, deciding whether we want to start a family, and choosing among various career opportunities. These choices will affect your life and the lives of those around you. It can be a lot to handle, especially when your friends are also experiencing the same doubts, fears, and mounting choices.

As we progress and change, so do our friendships. We're usually unable to provide the assistance or comfort that our friends have come to expect during these ups and downs. We're adjusting—or attempting to adjust—to the changing situations in our own lives, as well as to those in the lives of our friends. You may have decided to develop healthier habits, so you're devoting more time to exercise, sleep, and focusing on your needs. Simultaneously, your friend may need space to focus on herself and is, perhaps, studying for the bar examination or going to graduate school. You may have friends who move; it's difficult to lose them and learn how to cope with their absence, and it's especially challenging to try to figure out where the friendship stands after such a major change. Similarly, you may move and have to start making friends again. Or you may have a friend who travels a lot for her job—and that friend can be hard to keep track of.

Major life decisions about family, career, and who we want to become impact our friendships. If we feel isolated, sad, and lonely, there are good reasons for feeling that way. It's okay to acknowledge that the stress in our lives sometimes warrants a good old vent-fest. When the rug is being pulled out from under you, it's impossible not to fall over or to feel the heavy weight of gravity.

Situation 5: Friendships That Cannot Be Explained

How is it that we have friends we only see every couple of months, but every time you speak you're able to pick up right where you left off? How are such connections possible? I don't think there's an answer to this question. Those types of friends are amazing; they're usually the ones who leave us feeling positive and energized, and provide us with an instant, easy connection we may lack in other friendships. You can sit with each other after having lost contact for months, and you're comfortable; there's no pressure to fill the silence with words. The two of you can completely be yourselves with each other. Even though we don't see or talk to them regularly, we don't worry about the friendship.

I believe that everything happens for a reason, yet I also believe that people come in and out of our lives for inexplicable reasons. Another intriguing experience is meeting someone for the first time, and instantly feeling a powerful bond. I call this "friend-love at first sight." Such friendships develop fairly quickly, and it seems you're on the same page about everything. Perhaps it's similar backgrounds or experiences that create this effortless connection. It can be quite powerful and can lead to a deep friendship.

I experienced this phenomenon last year when I went to see a podiatrist after having pain in my right foot. After examination and subsequent treatment, he recommended a particular shoe store for new (and correct) exercise shoes. He also highly recommended that I see Stephanie, a former employee of his who had taken a job at the shoe store. So, I took his advice after being encouraged by the entire staff that I had to meet Stephanie and see how amazing she was. I was sort of curious; so I went there, met Stephanie, and felt an instant connection to her. I stayed at the store for about an hour and a half just talking to her. I usually don't talk to strangers that easily, but we both felt this unexplained link. We exchanged numbers and e-mails, have since kept in touch, and it seems effortless—even with our busy schedules. The timing was not the best, as I was preparing to move to another state; however, I don't worry about this special friendship because of the unspoken bond.

When I hear about women who have been friends for twenty or thirty years, I feel there must be some magical force driving the relationship. What's the secret to maintaining the friendship? How have you managed to stay friends through life's chaos and stresses? I also feel that perhaps something may be wrong with me because I haven't maintained a friendship for that long. How is it that some women remain close friends over decades, while other friendships last only two or three months?

Longtime friendships like these are truly confounding to me because I can't understand just how they have lasted for so long. However, I know they exist, and so they give me faith to keep on making new friends. They are the holy grails of friendship and cannot be explained. Perhaps these relationships spur us on to keep making friends because they're so inspiring. The relationships may not be as easy as they look on the outside, and I'm sure both parties continue to put in effort, but they have endured. This is what makes me hopeful that I can have friendships that last a lifetime—at least, that's my dream.

Situation 6: Something Has Changed in the Friendship

Another common situation is ceasing to feel comfortable around a friend because something seems to have changed without warning or explanation. It's hard to explain the shift, but it's something that makes interactions awkward or very different than they used to be. I believe that women have incredibly strong intuition; and so when there's an alteration in the friendship, one or both parties feel the change. That's another reason why friendships are more difficult for women—due to the deeper emotional connections, they pay more attention to their gut feelings. Women's intuition is not scientifically proven—but I've experienced it, and I'm sure you have, too.

Surviving Female Friendships: The Good, The Bad, and The Ugly
~ Nicole Zangara

These are somewhat the reverse of the friends we see only occasionally and the interactions remain stable. These are the friends who make us feel as though we're walking on eggshells when we spend time with them. There's a funny feeling that we can't shake or put into words, but we feel odd or think, *Well, that was weird.* Why do friendships change and how do we manage it? Do we tell the other person what we're feeling, or do we pretend that nothing has happened?

I experienced this when I went out to dinner with a longtime friend. It didn't take long to realize that the dynamic was not the same. She and I were in different places in our lives, which never seemed to matter before; now, suddenly, it did. The conversation flowed differently, and it felt harder to get on the same page. It was horrible—and it felt horrible. I was scared to admit this to myself at the time because I didn't want to lose the friendship. Such experiences can be hard to swallow, especially when it happens with a longtime friend.

Sometimes there's a reason for the change, like when friends move. I recently relocated to another state and found the reactions of friends interesting. I was curious to see which friends contacted me and which ones did not. It was also remarkable to see how friends handled the news of my move—which ones pulled away as the time grew near, and which ones wanted to spend more time with me. It was as if they realized how important the friendship was or how they truly felt about my leaving and wanted to get closer before my departure.

Moving creates a new dynamic because you may be used to seeing a friend once or twice a week and that's no longer possible. You may also wonder if you'll ever see a person again, whether the friendship is worth maintaining long distance, or if a friend misses you. This situation, too, sounds a lot like dating. I believe moving can strengthen a friendship; however, distance can cause a friendship to fizzle out if both people don't make an effort to keep it alive. It's possible that a friend is angry or resentful that you moved and doesn't want to hear about your new life; maybe you find it too difficult to keep up because you're focusing on building new friendships and relationships.

Changes, such as moving, are not easy roads to navigate. These events remind us and reinforce the fact that change is constant and can be difficult to manage. However, they can bring friends together—but it does require work on both ends. Maybe distance does make the heart grow fonder, and both of you work harder to stay in touch. It depends on the friendship and where each person is, emotionally and mentally.

I believe that we seek people going through similar experiences at any given time in our lives. So when you and a friend are in different emotional places, it's tricky to negotiate a level playing field. I rarely hear people openly discuss this change; comments tend to be, "We just stopped talking," or, "She's been really busy." When we stop communicating with a friend or interact less, and both parties seem to be okay with it, it's time to examine what's going on. Are you okay with letting the friendship go, or do you want to allow some time for it to return to normal? Friendships take on certain needs at certain times, and the friend we used to call every day to vent about job stress may not be the one to call after she changes jobs. The same is true of a friend with whom we no longer feel comfortable—maybe because our interests have changed or we feel less of a connection. I think these cycles happen a lot in friendships, yet they can be challenging to manage. Friendships are an investment and must be attended to.

Situation 7: The Friendship That Ends and You Have No Idea Why

We've all experienced having a friendship that lasts for years and then ends with no explanation. It's a struggle to understand what happened; and it's painful, especially if the friendship seemed strong and long-lasting. Many women don't discuss these stories because they feel embarrassed or ashamed. Who wants to talk about a heart-wrenching friendship breakup?

I'm not talking about friendships that fizzled out over time; rather, I'm referring to those that ended with finality. I have no clever answers as to why some women end a friendship without explanation, although I'm not sure what they'd say or do. Do you leave a note or tell the person why you're ending the friendship? It's the mature thing to do, but it may be difficult for both parties and it could cause more damage than needed.

We're emotional beings—but we're also reasonable, logical beings. This is why we try to make sense of nonsensical situations. We yearn to understand why someone would walk away from a long-standing friendship—and we also expect a good reason. Unfortunately, we're usually left waiting for that answer because it doesn't come; or worse, if we do get an answer later, it doesn't heal the wound or fill the void that's left. I believe these situations are among the worst of female friendships, because one person is left feeling vulnerable, angry, and confused.

Dana, a woman in her forties, has such a story. It's sad, and I had an emotional reaction to it because Dana is a very gentle and kind woman. She met Valerie at work, and while there was a slight age difference (Valerie was about ten years older than Dana), it didn't influence the friendship.

Their relationship developed slowly. Sometimes these are the most special, because you work on getting to know the person over time. Dana says it took a couple of years for them to acknowledge each other as good friends. Over the years, the two spent time together almost every day—taking walks in the morning and then having coffee afterwards. They also spoke on the phone many times during the day; sometimes to discuss something important, other times to say hello and share a funny thing that happened that day. Dana and Valerie were each other's confidants for almost eleven years.

When Dana got married, she noticed a shift in the friendship; Valerie seemed to be less available. They still saw each other, just not as often as they had, so the change didn't seem drastic. When Dana got pregnant, she looked forward to Valerie's advice and support because she was already a mother. To Dana's surprise, that didn't happen. In fact, Valerie stopped returning phone calls and it was practically impossible to get in touch with her. When they did talk, it was only on rare occasions, and soon they were not speaking at all. This was painful for Dana, and she didn't understand what was happening.

Dana was able to have a face-to-face conversation with Valerie who would only say the problem was not with Dana, but with her. Looking back, Dana still feels heartbroken and she asks herself what's wrong with her and what is it about her that a friend would give up so suddenly after so many years? This experience has made Dana look at all of her friends and wonder about the kind of people they are, almost as if she were taking a friend inventory and looking at each friend with a magnifying glass. This single experience made her doubt every other friendship she has ever had or has. When she shared these thoughts with me, I was at a loss for words.

Dana says that since that conversation, Valerie moved away and she's learned other things from her husband, including that Valerie's mother had passed away. Hearing this devastated Dana because, during their friendship, they'd turned to each other for support and comfort during such losses. For example, Valerie's husband, whom she was separated from, passed away, and Dana was there for Valerie during this time. So Dana was upset that she couldn't be there for Valerie in the way she wanted to be.

Looking back, Dana has come to her own conclusions about why the friendship ended the way it did. She believes that when she got married, she was not as available to Valerie, which may have been harder for Valerie than she realized. The friendship dynamics were changing; so when Dana's family was expanding and she was busier, Valerie had a hard time as her own family was crumbling due to losing her husband. But, even her guesses don't ease the pain she feels—and she's still left with more questions than answers.

Stories like Dana's may not provide insight as to why these situations happen, but they acknowledge that they do. People make choices; sometimes we never know why. This is especially troubling when the outcome is a break in the friendship. It's heartbreaking and can create a lot of self-doubt and confusion. We must recognize that we have the capability to hurt others with our decisions, and that's a risk we all take when entering a friendship.

Situation 8: Friends Dating and Breaking Up with Other Friends

What happens when a female friend dates one of our male friends and then they breakup? Turmoil, usually. It's not uncommon for friends in a given group to date each other or to have one night stands or flings; but when a serious relationship ends badly, it's difficult to know how to navigate the stormy waters. Can you stay neutral? Is it possible to stay friends with both?

Surviving Female Friendships: The Good, The Bad, and The Ugly
~ Nicole Zangara

I haven't figured this one out. But I have found that, in the end, you need to redefine boundaries and roles with each friend. You may have to set your own limits, for example, saying you will not discuss he- or she-who-will-not-be-named. It's challenging to plan future activities or gatherings when it may not be feasible to invite both parties. Then you're seen as the bad guy for choosing and becoming associated with the ex-partner. These situations often spiral downward and have the potential to end a friendship. Even though I like to think we all can act like adults, people's jealousy, anger, and sadness are intensified and can become difficult to manage.

If there is a divorce, it can be extremely difficult for friends to remain loyal to both parties; most choose one partner. I have witnessed this process and I'm sure you have, too. It would be nice to remain close with both people; but if the husband cheated and you were friends with the wife first, chances are you'll choose the wife and call the ex-husband a cheating SOB. True? It's nothing to joke about, but it can be interesting to watch how friends readjust around a divorced couple and try to find their new niche with each partner. Open communication can make the process go more smoothly.

Situation 9: The Friend Who Pops Back Into Your Life After You've Attempted Contact Without Success

We've all been there. We haven't spoken to a friend in months and tried to contact her with no response—and, then, suddenly we get an e-mail, phone call, or text inviting us somewhere or asking how we're doing. I have a tough time knowing how to respond. It's as if the person has no idea that it's been a long time and I may no longer consider her part of my inner circle; and that it's a bit strange to get an invitation after a considerable amount of time has passed.

Do you pretend that nothing has happened and pick up where you left off (which, by the way, may not be as great a place as the person remembers)? A friendship needs to be cared for by both people, and when someone disappears and reappears, an appropriate response requires some thought. When one party suddenly stops contact, it's hard not to feel some anger or resentment when you hear from them again, especially if you've tried to contact her without success.

If you consider the friendship worth rebuilding, do it. If not, you may not want to reinvest in the friendship, especially if the person allowed significant time to pass without considering you. Harsh? Maybe; but, those who reach out to you only when it's convenient for them are rude.

We all know people like this—ones who do things when they're good for them with no regard for anyone else's feelings. Where was this friend when you were trying to contact her? It may be convenient for her to suddenly come back into your life, but you don't have to allow her that access. This situation can be hard to manage; you may need to nip it in the bud, or give yourself time to figure out your next move.

Situation 10: Friends We Wonder About and/or Can't Stand

We all have friends who, when we see and/or talk with them, we silently ask ourselves, *Why am I friends with this person?* I'm not referring to an acquaintance, but to someone we would consider a friend. Why would we have a person like that in our lives?

Friends play different roles at different times in our lives, but I struggle with people who make us wonder how we became friends and why we're still friends. If you take a friend inventory, I'm sure you have one or more on your list. Maybe you worked together and continued the friendship, or perhaps you're friends with the same people and see each other at social functions.

The question gets tougher when you can't stand the person. Then I ask, "Why are you friends?" We all have an annoying friend, and/or one who's always immersed in drama—but there are also friends we really can't stand and yet we continue being friends with them. Why do we torture ourselves? Are we too ashamed to admit we can't be friends with everyone or that some people just rub us the wrong way? It's as if we're trying to prove something to ourselves by not making a change that may be needed. We may stay friends with someone out of convenience, or because it's too difficult to end the friendship. That's when we have to decide if we want to continue the friendship, or maybe re-evaluate the relationship and how it fits into our life. This is easier said than done; but if you can't come up with good enough reasons for being friends with someone, then that may be your answer.

Situation 11: A Friend's Partner Whom We Can't Stand

What about a close female friend who dates—and then marries—a jerk? Come on, you must be thinking of at least one person. While we're saying we adore our friend's partner, we may be thinking, *Oh no! How am I going to handle this awkward situation?* If you go out with your friend and she starts bringing her partner, you may be facing a difficult situation. I know people who have stopped spending time with certain friends for this reason. When I ask why they don't say something, they say, "Nicole, how do you tell your friend that you hate her husband?" Point taken.

This is a tough spot to be in because you don't want to give up the friendship, but dodging the partner can become increasingly difficult. For example, three couples I know, who are all in their fifties and sixties, are in this predicament; two of the women cannot stand the third woman's husband. As a result, they secretly make plans without the third woman because they don't want to invite her husband. It astonishes me that these things happen, but I'm not sure there's a right way to handle it. If someone doesn't like my partner, she shouldn't have to be around him; however, if my friend wants to continue being my friend, she has to find a way to manage her ill feelings. This, of course, is easier said than done.

Situation 12: Games We Play

We constantly test our friends—unconsciously, of course—to see how they will react. If you're always initiating phone calls or get-togethers, you may stop to see if your friend notices and/or contacts you. Similarly, if your friend is having a small gathering and you know you're not invited, you may text her to see what her plans are for that evening. Sneaky? Yes. We do this to see if our friends are, in fact, our friends. We do this because we're human, and have insecurities and fears of rejection and abandonment—but some of us become paranoid.

Here is the kicker: because we have so many modes of communication, including social media, we usually know what people are doing. Thus, when we learn we were left out of something, we become passive-aggressive or childish instead of up-front and honest. I believe this doesn't happen on a conscious level, but sometimes we're so afraid of the truth that we Facebook-stalk or ask other friends what's going on instead of going to the source. It's exhausting to play these games, and yet we continue to do so; maybe it's some masochistic trait, or we enjoy the thrill of the game. Who knows?

Everyone wants to be secure in their friendships. But when there's evidence that a friend may not be who we think she is, we become insecure. Some women take this a step further and become paranoid. This may be triggered by previous negative experiences with friends. This leads to game-playing and testing friends' loyalty. For those who don't play games, I applaud your confidence in your friendships.

Situation 13: Competitive Friends

Do you have a friend who always has to one-up you or is always talking about her next great vacation? There are those for whom being eternally in the spotlight seems to be their life's goal—and this can create competition in the friendship. Females are tricky, and so when one friend starts eating healthier and training for a marathon, the other may start to feel fat and lazy. I've been on the other side of this scenario—I'm a gym rat, and I've noticed that when some of my friends start exercising or engage in some healthy activity, they feel a need to tell me. It's as if they're reporting what they did in return for a prize. Of course, I'm happy for them, but I find it interesting that gym visits suddenly become a topic of conversation. I can understand and appreciate their need to connect, but when a friend begins sending text messages to me about her daily workouts, it just seems silly and unnecessary.

Have you ever played a game with a friend and, suddenly, you fear for your life because she becomes a monster totally focused on winning—and the prize is a stuffed teddy bear? Some competition is healthy; however, when some friends always have to share their latest accolades, it can become unpleasant.

How would you approach this type of friend? Would it be worth it? What would you say? Chances are this person knows she's like this, but no one has had the courage to say anything to her. So you need to ask yourself if you want someone like this in your life. If, when you leave this friend, you feel worse about yourself, something is wrong. But maybe there are activities you do together that you enjoy, or you feel she's better in one-on-one situations rather than in a group. Finding the positive qualities in these friends can help strengthen the relationship. However, if you start feeling as if you have to buy a new car for no other reason than because she did, please count to five, put the check book down, and walk away.

Situation 14: Singledom

As I get older, I find it more difficult to "get out there," especially since I work full time and I'm trying to keep up with bills, laundry, and sleep. When you have friends who still like to go out—and you may not—you are seen as someone who's not social. I feel weird when I go out to clubs and see females who are in their early twenties wearing what seems like a piece of cloth for an outfit. For me, fun social events are going out to dinner, hanging out with friends at a coffee shop or someone's house, and/or going out for a glass of wine. I'm no longer interested in being in a crowded club. If you enjoy that scene, I promise I won't judge.

I may sound as if I'm complaining, but as single women (myself included) get older, it's harder to be social because the things we used to do are no longer available or enticing. It also becomes more difficult to meet people—and I think this applies at any age. Any woman can struggle to find fun activities if she hasn't found the right group of people to do these activities with. I empathize with other single women because it can be overwhelming and daunting to get out and be social, especially if you feel limited in what you can do and with whom.

If you have young female friends, they may still be in the club/bar scene and want to get drunk and go home with the cute guy. I, on the other hand, like to sit in my pajamas, catching up on the backlog on my DVR. However, it's important to spend time with friends, so it's about finding balance. Perhaps joining a cooking class or a book club is appealing, or you can tell your friends that you'd like to go out, but suggest having a dinner party instead.

I get tired of hearing from friends that I never go out; because in their minds, that means going out to a club until two o'clock in the morning. I go out to dinner and/or watch movies with my friends—and I find that enjoyable.

Surviving Female Friendships: The Good, The Bad, and The Ugly
~ Nicole Zangara

I recently overheard a conversation in which a woman—who was probably in her mid-thirties—was recounting how she'd started training for marathons because it was a good excuse why she couldn't go out and/or be out late on the weekends. She also said it was a good excuse not to drink and that people didn't give her a hard time about it. I found it interesting that this woman felt she had to give her friends excuses and, on top of that, she felt badly that she wasn't doing the activities they were. I sympathized, because I feel I've been in that situation and it's unpleasant.

The fact that we feel like we have to give people excuses is worth examining. Do we not feel confident enough to say, "Listen, I just want to stay in tonight. I don't feel like going out." Is that so bad? I've been given a hard time by friends when I do go out, and get comments such as, "Nicole, you're alive!" or "You do exist!" I laugh it off and try to play it cool—but I get irritated because there are other ways to see people than going out to a club/bar. I see those I want to see and call those I want to talk to—and that's fine with me.

Instead of getting defensive, giving excuses, or laughing it off, it's important to say what you really mean. Try it and see what happens. Your friends may tease you or make snide comments, but that tells you what type of people they are. If a friend says, "Oh, thank goodness! I'm glad you don't want to go out. Let's go get a bite to eat instead!" then I would say that person is a keeper. I challenge you to be honest and not give excuses, especially to your friends. Being single isn't a crime, so stop punishing yourself.

Situation 15: Perceptions and First Impressions

The discussion about perceptions and how two people can have very different ones in a friendship is an interesting one. I've thought a relationship was fine until the friend tells me thoughts and feelings she's had; maybe we're out to dinner, and she shares that she's been holding on to anger about a comment I made at the last party we attended. Or I think I'm very close to a friend I've known for a year, and she later says that she didn't think of me as a close friend until only recently. Perceptions are tricky because we live in our own realities and see things through our own sets of goggles. I may think the friend is mad at me because she's been taking longer than usual to respond to my calls and texts, when she may think I'm mad at her. This is where the stereotype of female drama gets its ugly reputation. Instead of discussing misperceptions, many friends continue on until they're so uncomfortable that they have to confront the problem. Or instead of confronting the friend, they ask other friends if something is wrong. We dance around the problem instead of going straight to the source.

When the discussion does happen, it can open up the dialogue and create deeper connections and understanding. I experienced a situation in which there were such negative feelings about something that took place with a friend that I stopped talking to her—out of anger—for over a year. When I got up the courage to e-mail her, she responded, "Oh, I just figured that with time and distance we grew apart." I thought she was mad at me, and I was hurt, but during all that time, she assumed the friendship had run its course. This is why it's important—no, it's life or death to a friendship—that people discuss their perceptions because they're often incorrect. Yes, there are instances when a friend is mad at you for flirting with the guy she likes or for talking to her ex-husband, but women frequently assume way too much. Instead of perceiving, talk first!

Another example is when you and a friend become close, and then share your first impressions, which may have been quite negative. Paula, a woman in her forties, has had experience with this phenomenon. Paula has a friend, Ruth, whom she met through her daughter. Paula's first impression of Ruth was that of a woman always dressed to the nines. Ruth was smart and beautiful, and she'd always invited

Paula to events and made her feel welcome. The two scheduled a play date for their daughters; even the little girls seemed to have a special bond.

As Paula and Ruth began to spend more time together, they discussed their first impressions of each other. The conversation was prompted by their trying to remember how they met and became friends. Ruth said she thought Paula was a snob; Paula replied that she thought Ruth was uptight. Although they laughed, it made them realize that had they believed those first impressions, they may have not become close friends.

Stories like Paula's are important because most of us have experienced a negative first impression or interaction, and later this person becomes your best friend. First impressions matter, but they also demonstrate that we may change our minds over time. For example, we may think someone comes across as too opinionated, but we begin to admire her outgoing and strong personality. Perceptions and first impressions are interesting because things are not always what they seem. It's important to have an open mind when meeting potential friends, because you never know who will end up being with you for life.

Situation 16: Loss and Friendships

We all experience loss, and we see death happen more often as we grow older. It's part of life, and one that can be painful and earth shattering. I was lucky enough to not experience a major death until I was in my mid-twenties, when my beloved grandmother died from pancreatic cancer. It was heartbreaking, and I was thankful to have my family to lean on. However, a lot of my friends didn't know what to say or how to act. When friends experience loss, it can trigger memories of our own losses, and we may distance ourselves without realizing what we're doing.

I received the news at work, before lunchtime; I told some co-workers what had happened. I was sitting in the break room eating my lunch and trying to process the news, when somehow the topic turned to death. I have no idea why it did, and I was in no condition to even begin to understand. I started to cry, quickly left the room, and began to sob. I had a wonderful supervisor who came to the room I found refuge in and hugged me for a few minutes. I know my co-workers didn't mean to hurt me, but I couldn't understand why they would discuss death after just hearing the news about my grandmother. In retrospect, I have a greater understanding of why this topic came up; it may have reminded them of their own losses, personal or professional, and they may have felt it was appropriate to discuss their experiences. For me, it was just too much to handle at that moment.

Sometimes individuals who are typically caring, sweet, and good-natured don't know how to act around people who've experienced loss, nor do they know how to manage grief. Death is an uncomfortable subject, and it's not easy to sit with someone else's pain, especially if you haven't managed your own.

However, two friends, one male and one female, went above and beyond the call of duty during this period. When I flew back after the funeral, Brandon was nice enough to drive me home from the airport (remember Lacy and her thoughts about the airport? I could not agree more). Unbeknownst to me, he'd invited my close female friend, Michelle, to accompany him. I believe Brandon's surprising me with Michelle was intended to make me less sad because he knew the history of my friendship with Michelle—and he thought her presence would cheer me up. When he picked me up, I was both happy and surprised to see her. That experience will stay with me forever, and it meant so much that they were both there for me. I was feeling such loss and pain that it was refreshing and consoling to see two people whom I care for be so concerned about me. That is how true friendship should feel, and I'll forever be grateful to them for making such a profound loss a little less painful.

When a woman loses her partner, her world changes. Friends may not know how to console her or how to continue on in the friendship—or how to deal with their own grief. However, Claudia, a woman in her fifties, told me a positive story about loss and friendship.

Claudia and her husband had many friends who were couples that they socialized with frequently. When her husband passed away thirteen years ago, Claudia's life changed drastically, as did some of those friendships. Of the many couples she and her husband knew, only a few remained in her circle of friends. After the funeral, her mother told her that things would change, and that some friends would no longer be there for her. But she also reminded Claudia that she would meet new friends, which was as true as her first statement.

Claudia did indeed gain a new friend. One of her daughters' classmates learned of her husband's death, and ran home to tell his mother the sad news. This young boy, Kevin, wanted to do something for Claudia and her family. He gave gifts to Claudia's daughter, which meant a great deal to Claudia. Kevin's mother, Roxanne, and Claudia didn't know each other well; the only interaction they'd had involved Claudia saying something stupid regarding a surgery Roxanne had just had. According to Claudia, it was not her finest hour.

Claudia called Roxanne, to say thank you—and their conversation lasted almost an hour. Roxanne shared her own experience with grief and loss—her own mother had passed away—and so she was all too aware of the feelings of loss and heart-wrenching emotions one goes through when a loved one dies. Even though a parent's death is different than a spouse's, the feelings of grief are similar; and so Claudia not only felt instantly connected to, but also felt as if she'd found a source of support in Roxanne.

Roxanne continued to be supportive as Claudia and her family attended a bereavement group. One night after the group-meeting ended, Roxanne stopped by Claudia's house with some ice cream. Claudia was dealing with her own feelings and trying to be strong for her children; and it was little acts of kindness like this one that consoled her. Although the two don't see each other every day, they still have some great rituals. For example, when Roxanne travels, she brings gifts back for Claudia; and every holiday season, Claudia takes Roxanne homemade cake. They look forward to these events and expect that the other one will always come through.

Surviving Female Friendships: The Good, The Bad, and The Ugly
~ Nicole Zangara

Claudia says she and Roxanne are very different, yet tragedy brought them together and they now have a strong bond. When telling others this story, they say that Claudia's husband brought them together even though Roxanne had never met him. Claudia values this genuine friendship deeply.

Stories like Claudia's give us hope and faith in times of darkness and despair. Had Roxanne's son not been so touched by a classmate's story and not told his mother, these women would probably not have met or developed the intense bond they share today. During—and after—a major life change, friendships don't always remain constant, and the people we used to count on may no longer be our anchors. Friendships are always being tested, much like marriage vows—in sickness and in health, among other things—and some friends bolt when the going gets rough.

Death and loss are difficult life experiences, and will affect a friendship and all those involved. The only advice I can give is that we need to do what's right for us in order to protect our feelings. Sometimes another's loss can trigger memories of our own losses and we may need to pull back to get some space. However, discuss your feelings with your friends so they are aware of the reasons for your distance.

Communication is the key in any relationship, so telling a friend what you're feeling is okay. She may not understand or accept what you're thinking or feeling, but at least you're sharing what's going on with you. We all deal with grief and loss in different ways; and so every friendship will weather such storms uniquely. The story above illustrates how friendships can be created out of loss and can help overcome that loss; how people can be brought together by something painful and later share something beautiful.

Situation 17: Hot, Cold, and Mean Friends

Throughout my friendship experiences, I have the hardest time staying friends with women who run hot and cold. Let me explain. Do you know women who are sweet one day, then are short with you the next? I understand that we experience a range of emotions, and that our behavior is not one hundred percent consistent. However, when your friend leaves you feeling puzzled about whether she likes you or is irritated with you, and this happens on a daily basis, you may want to reconsider the friendship. When friends are one day Jekyll and the next day Hyde, it's hard to know which end is up. Friendships are intricate enough, so to be wondering what mood a friend will be in from day-to-day becomes overwhelming.

Moreover, I've heard women say they have friends who are "kind of mean and nasty." First, I wonder if they're implying that she's opinionated or direct. The answer I usually get is, "No, she's kind of a ____ (use your imagination with this adjective)." Again, why are you friends with this person? Am I crazy for asking this question? I don't think so. What is the allure of mean friends? Frankly, spending time with nasty people is not my first choice.

Perhaps this friend has other qualities that are positive, and her meanness is just one of many. Maybe she feels like she can have a no-holds-barred attitude with you, so she lets down all her defenses and has no filter. Another guess is that you're torturing yourself and you need to end that friendship.

I'm not sure I could stick out a friendship with a mean woman. I'd be too sensitive to her remarks and probably feel worse about myself and the friendship. Nonetheless, it intrigues me when a friend tells me about her cruel friends, especially if I view her as the nicest woman I've ever met.

Situation 18: A Man Disrupts the Friendship

I saved this one for last because, unfortunately, it's an experience many women go through, and one that deserves

119

attention. This can take many forms—having a crush on the same guy, secretly dating our best friend's ex, and/or getting involved with a friend's husband and/or boyfriend. These situations are the worst; one can foresee the massive explosion ahead.

Why is it that, even though we know the outcome and consequences, we still do these things? Are there not unwritten codes between friends that dictate, *Thou shalt not date your best friend's ex, or like the same guy*? Men have these codes of conduct ("bros before hos"), so I know they exist. The unspoken rule between female friends is that when a guy comes along, the women try to prevent him from disrupting their friendship. But let's be honest—that's difficult. We sometimes do let our emotions get the best of us and think with our hearts, desires, and hormones—not our minds.

I experienced this in high school. I had a huge crush on Todd—and my friend, Melissa, did, too—although I was unaware of her feelings. Todd and I had been spending time together, but I wasn't ready to move the relationship forward because I didn't really know him. Later, I was told by another friend that Melissa and Todd had shared an intimate kiss (and most likely did more than just kiss) one weekend while I was away. I was heartbroken—and I lost my respect for and trust in Melissa. I felt deceived, angry, and all of the other emotions you'd expect. Oddly, I was more upset with Melissa than Todd because, as women, we have lower expectations for the guy. The female should know better. I remember discussing the situation with Melissa and found no sincerity in her apology. I could tell that deep down she really didn't care how I felt. It was a harsh experience, yet it provided me with insight about how cold women can be, as well as what can happen when a guy enters the picture.

I don't believe that any woman, no matter how awful, sets out looking to steal a friend's crush or partner. Best friends care about each other's feelings; but when a cute, smart, and funny guy comes along, it's hard not to become competitive if you're both interested. If he chooses your friend, you can feel devastated and insecure. Why did he choose her? Why can't I get the guy? What is it about me? And seeing them together is a constant reminder of what you could have had—what you're not having. It strains the friendship and it's rarely acknowledged or discussed openly. How would you approach this?

Female friends want to believe they'd never, ever let a man get in the way—but that's just not true. I think we have the best intentions, but when a guy enters a friendship equation, things can get dicey. I don't mean that I think women who do this are right (I don't), but these situations are, unfortunately, very common.

Some friendships may fall apart under this stress because if you're not chosen, it can be painful to see your crush and best friend together. In this situation, taking the high road may mean protecting your feelings—try to not let it bother you—but it still feels horrible, and you have to make a choice between continuing the friendship or walking away. Sometimes it's tough to get back to normal when feelings are raw. It's sad that a friendship can deteriorate so easily when a guy enters the picture.

That is why it is so important to communicate. It may not be the most fun conversation, but it can only help the friendship and provide insight regarding how strong it is. If you both agree on how to handle yourselves around this oh-so-amazing guy by mutually deciding not to pursue him, that may work. That may require some super-woman strength from both of you, but if the friendship is more important, you have the answer. Or maybe one of you says "go for it," and means it.

Many complicated situations occur in a friendship, and it's hard to know how to manage things without overreacting, causing a rift, losing the friend, or losing your mind. I find all of these situations more difficult as I get older, and something tells me it won't get easier.

The take-away from this chapter is not for you to think, "Great, now I'm even *more* depressed about my friendships." The goal is for you to see how easily friendships can lose steam when you and your friend are not putting in the effort, and that there are many factors that require special attention and care. Friendships ebb and flow, and are unpredictable. They constantly change because of our own changes—jobs, personal choices, and overall outlook on life. When a friend starts dating someone we despise, that may pose as a problem; when she responds less to our calls, then it may be worth addressing this behavior.

Complex situations happen in any friendship. It's about making sure that we're talking about these complexities so that the friendship can continue to grow in a positive manner. It's a lot like dancing with a partner; you don't want to step on his/her toes, but it's inevitable in the beginning. Together, you make mistakes while learning the moves, as well as how to be with one another. Once you're in a good rhythm, the fun truly begins!

Wendy: A Woman in Her 60s

Wendy begins her story in the 1970s, when feminism was gaining momentum. She considers those times unique, because women were learning to come together and fight for their rights. She says that women came together because of their values and recognition of their aggregate power in their struggle for individuality and freedom.

Wendy's female friendships have influenced not only her values, but also how she sees herself today. She remembers women she's known who helped shape her outlook on life and taught her to build friendships on trust, respect, and acceptance. When this foundation is lacking or either person has insecurities, problems ensue, and one has an enemy rather than a friend. Wendy has also learned that while some women can bring you down, there are other women who will help you back up.

Wendy's experience is about both of these types of friends. She met Katherine, who moved to the area where Wendy lived. The goal was to welcome her and her family and to help with any questions she had about the community. Both their husbands were in the same business and they both traveled frequently for work. As a result, the two women spent more time together. However, Wendy soon found out that her husband and Katherine were involved. The fact that the two had supported each other through losses made the pain overwhelming for Wendy.

Many of Wendy's friends, however, would not let her wallow in her sorrow, and were there for her—making sure her children were cared for and helping her find good lawyers, doctors, and real estate agents. They were the guiding force and strength that she needed. Wendy is still grateful, in part, because her children saw firsthand the power of the female bond and how friends support each other when one is dealing with grief and pain. She has witnessed the benefits of those friendships based on trust, respect, and acceptance.

ഇ Chapter Nine ര

The Media and Friendships

Settle in again, because I will now explore the media and our favorite television shows and movies. (I will not discuss reality television because, in my opinion, it's not reality.) When I watch shows like *Sex and the City* (*SATC*) or *Friends*, it's difficult not to get wrapped up in the fictional lives of these people. They make it look so easy. Who doesn't want to be friends with the fabulous girls from *SATC* and/or the wild, fun group from *Friends*? The friendships on these shows seem genuine and loving—two critical characteristics. It's hard not to want the same types of friendships in our own lives, especially if you grew up watching these shows.

The reality is, however, that friendships are not this predictable or constant. All these fictional unions seem to last, which begs the question—is that possible? Even though there are fights, which are usually worked through, is the portrayal realistic? I hope that we're all capable of having friendships like the ones seen on *SATC* and *Friends*, yet I question the longevity. Is it realistic to think that four women can remain such close friends over ten-to-fifteen years, despite family, jobs, and daily life responsibilities? I would like to think that it's possible because it would be wonderful to have people like that in our lives. And the same with *Friends*. Is it likely that a group of men and women could be that close and, at the same time, live with each other without needing personal space? I remain optimistic that friendships can last, but I wonder if this issue is fairly represented in the media.

The media does a careful, sneaky job creating these fantasy lives and we become hooked—and then invested—in the characters on the show. In college, friends and I gathered to watch *SATC*. It was a major event, one that required planning, and anyone who dared talk during the show was quickly reprimanded. We felt connected to the characters, and often someone would say that she identified with Carrie or Samantha. *SATC* brought my real-life friends together. So, that was a positive, as well as it being an example of how the media can provide positive opportunities for friends to get together, put down their cell phones, and enjoy watching a television show or movie.

How does the media portray friendships? Is it done realistically or is it a fantasy that we aspire to and/or mimic so we can have what they have? Well, we create our own standards, but the media certainly influences them. I grew up watching *Beverly Hills, 90210*, and have fond memories of watching it with my brothers. The group of characters made me hope for friends like Donna, Kelly, and Brenda. Was that a good or bad thing? I don't know. But I was addicted to the show and still catch reruns on TV occasionally.

The media plays a huge role in how we conceive our likes and dislikes. From reality shows to drama and comedy, we tend to find something in a character we can identify with. For example, the *SATC* characters' lives and relationships are alluring to the viewer. However, I worry about this portrayal and how it lays the foundation for what we aspire to. Of course, we can discern between reality and fantasy, but sometimes the line between the two becomes blurred.

Television shows and/or movies don't always accurately depict what happens when your best friend moves, or when there's a falling out. For instance, in the second *SATC* movie, was it realistic that Samantha was able to fly to New York City so often to visit her friends? Sure, one could argue that she traveled for her job but I wonder how that would work in real life. Obviously, though, many shows wouldn't last if they accurately portrayed real life.

Many young women grow up watching these shows and are affected by what the show is selling. The friendships always work out and there's always a happy ending, but that doesn't really happen. Can you honestly say that friends could fight—and make up—in thirty or sixty minutes? We're not prepared for that reality and it can be tough to face.

To be fair, I will say that the second *SATC* movie did a better job showing how friends deal with distance, family, and work conflicts. It realistically portrayed life changes and how they impact friendships. For example, it was clear that Charlotte was just short of having a nervous breakdown trying to deal with the stress of being a mother and she felt her friends wouldn't understand and would possibly judge her if they knew her true feelings about motherhood. Similarly, Samantha was living in a different state and trying to manage her relationship, job, and missing her friends, while facing a decision about what and who was most important. Carrie's situation was the usual mess and it always came down to trying to keep her best girlfriends in her life and dealing with Big, her complicated on-again, off-again love throughout the show. Last but not least, there's Miranda, the high-powered lawyer who continually struggled to balance her career and relationships. All of the characters act out some real-life dilemmas for real women.

Another movie worth discussing is *Bridesmaids*, because it positively and accurately portrays female friendships. Lillian, the main character, is getting married, and the other female characters are trying to process and adjust to what that means. Annie and Lillian are best friends, and the audience watches Annie struggle with Lillian's new life, new husband, and new friends. The story is told through Annie, which allows people to identify with the loss and sadness of a changing friendship.

Annie is also dealing with Lillian's friendship with Helen and what that means for her; there are some hysterically funny scenes, especially the one where Annie and Helen are trying to top one another with toasting the bride-to-be at the engagement party. It's clear that Annie feels threatened by Helen and vice-versa, as they fight for the BFF title.

Many women, including me, cried and laughed throughout the movie, sometimes simultaneously, because we understood and felt for Annie. The powerful bond between Annie and Lillian is always evident, and we feel

130

their grief regarding the changes that will take place. Even when conflict arose, Annie and Lillian confronted each other and spoke honestly about their feelings, which led to resolution and an open conversation about their fears. *Bridesmaids* did a wonderful job depicting the female friendship realistically and was also a beautiful portrayal of female attachments.

A movie that examines the intrusion of a man into a best friendship is *Something Borrowed*. Darcy and Rachel, the main characters, are best friends and have known each other all their lives. Dex, the intruding male, was Rachel's friend in law school, and becomes Darcy's fiancé. Rachel introduces Darcy and Dex, and then pretends not to care when they express interest in each other, despite Rachel having feelings for Dex.

The film portrays the complicated dynamics of being in love with your best friend's fiancé. On the night of Rachel's surprise thirtieth birthday party, she and Dex end up sleeping together. Through Rachel, the audience experiences the pain of being torn between her best friend and the man she thought she could never have. The ending (spoiler alert) shows Rachel and Darcy having an amicable conversation on a sidewalk, but the audience is left thinking that their friendship didn't survive—which is realistic. I'm not sure I would have believed their relationship would have survived—even given their long-standing history—because of the broken trust that occurred.

Also, although what Rachel did was wrong, the audience roots for her to end up with Dex because she never does what she wants and always gives in, demonstrated through her friendship with Darcy. In the end, Rachel gets what she wants by realizing she wasn't living the life she wanted, which makes her stronger. She even sets boundaries with Darcy. *Something Borrowed* realistically shows the chaos that can occur when there are secrets between the best of friends, and how those secrets can hurt the friendship, as well as how love can complicate—and even break—the female bond.

A television show that I think is brilliantly written is *New Girl*. Jess, the protagonist, is living with three single guys after breaking up with her boyfriend. There is, of course, drama, but one episode focuses on Jess's friendship with her best friend, Cece. Jess is finally told that Cece and one of Jess' male roommates, Schmidt, have been sleeping together. Jess is obviously upset and hurt by the news, and tries to avoid and ignore Cece, albeit in funny ways. What seems to bother Jess the most is that she thought the two told each other everything. During a heated scene, Cece lets Jess know that's not true, then proceeds to tell her that she stopped telling Jess all her secrets because when she did, Jess was critical and judged her. Cece stopped sharing, and then let Jess be the one to do that.

There are many teaching moments from that one interaction. First, Jess learned that she perceived the friendship as both being open and honest with each other, which wasn't entirely true. Second, Jess is trying to understand Cece's feelings for Schmidt, which brings up the issue of friends dating our male friends, and the chaos that can ensue if it ends badly. Third, it allows us to see how friends handle a fight and that there can be (and is) resolution—in this case, both sharing their feelings (Jess's hurt and Cece's fear of judgment) and moving forward in a positive direction. Although this whole process would've taken more than thirty minutes, it's not too far off from what this situation would look like in real life.

From *Friends* to *Sex and the City* to *Beverly Hills, 90210*, television and movies provide a variety of depictions of female friendships. Some are realistic, while others present a fantasy of perfect female friendship—which may be what's so alluring to the viewer. We always want what we can't have, so the media gives us what we want every day. Thankfully, some television shows and movies do a more realistic job in validating our feelings as we laugh at the main characters, whose pain we have felt at some point in our own lives.

So ask yourself this about your favorite show and/or movie: how would these characters fare in real life, with real problems? Would they survive? My guess is that they wouldn't—and then the screen would fade to black and the credits would start to roll. And why are women so addicted to shows that sell fantasy sisterhood? Do we want to feel that we're a part of something because we haven't had that experience ourselves?

I challenge you to get a group of your friends together to discuss these questions. On the one hand, you may be surprised to know which television shows and/or movies your friends like; on the other hand, it may stimulate an interesting discussion about these television shows and/or movies. In reality (outside of your HDTV), it takes work and commitment to sustain a friendship. You can't fast-forward through life's commercials, nor can you press pause when things get a little too heated with a friend.

When you need a good laugh or some mindless entertainment, watching your favorite television show or movie can be a great outlet. I'm not advising you to stop watching TV, but it becomes an issue if you're going to your

TV for comfort, or wishing you had the types of friendships you see on the television screen.

The next time you're watching a show or a movie, be aware of your thoughts and reactions, as well as how drawn in you get to the drama. I also encourage you to think about how you'd handle the issue at hand. My guess is that you may have a newfound appreciation for real-life relationships, and that's something the media can't give you.

๑ Chapter Ten ๙

Facebook

Facebook is intriguing, yet absolutely annoying. I became a Facebook user in college. It's become something everyone seems to be using—including my mother, and probably yours, too. It has changed over the years, so now you can update your status, send a message, and post something on your friend's wall—all in under one minute.

Because of my fascination and irritation with Facebook, I'll address four situations I find common when using it. There are many more; however, I wish to focus on what I believe is the most common.

Surviving Female Friendships: The Good, The Bad, and The Ugly
~ Nicole Zangara

Situation 1: Discovering Important Information About Your Friends

One of the best things about using Facebook (heavy sarcasm) is discovering things about your friends. Not the fact that a friend went to a movie or bought the latest, most awesome Groupon deal. I'm talking about big things. The best example is finding out that a close female friend is engaged. I've experienced this, so I know how it feels to log on to Facebook and read that type of wall post as if it's not a big deal. It's bizarre to find out that a close friend's relationship status has changed in this way, especially when it's as important as an engagement. Is this how we communicate now? Do we have so many friends (I'm talking to the 500-plus club) that we need to post something major to let all of them know—even those we consider close friends? Do you really talk to all those friends? If you do, then you must be extremely tired and need a long vacation.

However, before I continue, I will assume that some of you who do (or have done) this did call those few friends you consider close to share the news. At least, I hope that's true.

I wish there were more consideration and sensitivity when friends post significant information, especially when it would be more meaningful to find out in person or over the phone. Besides, isn't it exciting to hear a friend's voice when she's sharing the news? What about when you can't wait to call your friend and squeal together like little girls? Or better yet, when we say, "There's something I want to share, and I want to wait until I can tell you in person!" Those moments are priceless. To those friends who have called us to tell us their news, I say, "Good job!" They took an extra step to think about you and the importance of friendship. For those who posted their news, I wonder how you'd feel if the shoe were on the other foot.

Finding out information about a close friend on Facebook can make you feel dismissed, minimized, and as if you're the last to know. It can bring up insecurities and feelings of rejection from other friendship experiences. We start to question the friendship and whether that person thinks of us as a good friend—and it can create some major doubts. Granted, it could be nothing and the friend just didn't think of contacting certain people, but it's worth acknowledging the feelings that can so easily be brought out in all of us. Facebook does a great job of taking us back to high school shenanigans. Didn't we already experience that? This isn't *Lost*; we don't want to go back to the island.

Using Facebook to share information with our family and friends is a good thing; I just have to wonder what information we're sharing and why. Is it important that we let everyone know we're sitting on the couch eating a bag of chips? And the reverse—casually posting that you're pregnant, engaged, and/or won the Nobel Peace Prize? There's a difference in the value of the news and what it means to your family and friends. Maybe it's more convenient to post information because it saves the time it would take to make a phone call or tell someone face-to-face. I wonder why posting major news is becoming the norm.

In addition, how are you doing all of these amazing, life-altering things if you're posting about them every five minutes? This stumps me—and I laugh about it when I see post after post after post. The post should be, "I'm posting on Facebook," because that's what you're doing. Okay. Let's continue.

Situation 2: Finding Out About Events You Were Not Invited To

Another sticky situation is finding out there was an event that all of your friends attended—and you weren't invited. Maybe this is considered Facebook stalking; but when friends post pictures or activities on their walls and mention or tag these activities with other friends, it's not hard to figure out what happened and wonder why you weren't included.

Let's be fair and give your friends some credit; you don't always know the reasons why you weren't included, and it doesn't help to make assumptions. Hopefully you have enough faith in your friends to know that they're not malicious and wouldn't intentionally hurt you. People often post pictures of events on Facebook not to be cruel, but to share their experiences; the idea is connection. However, I wish people were more mindful of what they post and how it may affect others' feelings. A common example is a message like this: "Out on the town with my faves!" My first reaction to this is: *Really? So whoever was not out on the town with you is not your fave?* Petty, perhaps, but when people post what they're doing and with whom, it's hard not to have some type of reaction. That is why I am trying to use Facebook less as I get older, although now it seems as though people my age are using it more. Go figure.

Olivia, whom we met earlier, found pictures on Facebook of friends at another friend's birthday party. She wasn't invited and had no idea about it. A few months before this incident, Olivia invited Grace (the birthday girl) and this group of women to her birthday party and had been staying in contact—and regularly getting together— with them.

Surviving Female Friendships: The Good, The Bad, and The Ugly
~ Nicole Zangara

Needless to say, when she saw these pictures, she was hurt. Why wasn't she invited to—or at least told about—the event? Did she have to see pictures of her friends having a good time without her? She talked to Grace a few months later, but nothing came of it. Grace didn't acknowledge Olivia's feelings nor apologize. By that time, Olivia really disliked Facebook and realized there are some negative aspects to using it. She was confused, as she'd known these women for almost twenty years. Sometimes ignorance is bliss.

Olivia's story illustrates how hurtful it can be to see posts and pictures of your friends smiling and having a good time—especially if you didn't know about the event. Again, it seems there's too much accessibility on Facebook and people post way too much information. Of course, it's nice to see what a friend is up to, but sometimes I feel like a voyeur. In about five seconds, I'm overloaded with information about family and friends. I struggle with the lack of privacy, although I've figured out how to activate all of the necessary privacy options. All I ask is for people to be more sensitive to what they post and the information they're publically sharing, especially if someone who should have been a part of it is not.

Situation 3: Friending and De-friending

De-friending, when you remove someone from your friends list on Facebook, is the most interesting—yet cruel—way to end a friendship, especially if you expect to see that person at some time again. I'm guilty of this, as I've de-friended a few people; however, I can rationalize why I did so. Nonetheless, when you're on the other side of the de-friending (the de-friendee), it can seem childish especially when you have no idea why the person did it (Facebook is sneaky enough that you won't know you've been de-friended unless you search the person's name). How would you address that topic? I can just imagine it. "Hi, Ashley, how's it going? I wouldn't know because you de-friended me on Facebook!" Or, "Hi, Ashley, how did it feel to de-friend me on Facebook?" I assume you're thinking, *Really? Get over it.* Yet, you'd be surprised to know how many people de-friend and/or get de-friended, and then have to deal with the consequences—like running into the person and facing public humiliation and/or awkward conversation.

Another way to examine this topic is to ask: what constitutes de-friending? I'm curious about why people de-friend. Do you no longer feel the person is even an acquaintance? Or did something happen between you two, and there's such a low probability that you'll run into her that you thought, *Why not?* Maybe you went through your friend list, found you can't stand some of the people, and thought, "Time to de-friend!" Conversely, I know women who have de-friended each other, worked through the problem, and then re-friended. I think there should be an extra Facebook security step if you de-friend someone, and then decide to become friends again. Would it be worthwhile if you had to jump through hoops to re-friend the person?

Moreover, if the friendship ended on bad terms, it's interesting to see who will de-friend first; it's inevitable, since the two of you probably no longer want to have anything to do with each other. It becomes a race to be the one to de-friend, as if you're rushing to be the first to make the statement, "This friendship is over. Period." De-friending is another way of taking this person out of your life, and may happen after you've deleted her information from your contact list. This can be very cathartic and, if you haven't experienced this yet, I'm sure you will.

Something I don't understand, however, is when women whom no longer consider each other friends stay Facebook friends as a way to see what the other is up to. Why do women do this? You don't like each other, you don't talk to each other, so why do you want to know what the other is doing? Some women have shared that their curiosity gets the best of them, and/or they want the woman to know what they're doing, as if to say, "Hey, look at me. I'm happy without you." While I can understand this to a degree, it seems as if you're hurting yourself by seeing this friend pop up on your news feed. This can trigger feelings which, I'm guessing, are not positive. Additionally, it's unhealthy not to let this friendship go, as it's not providing any benefits. This situation is comparable to the breakup of a romantic relationship, and how some women continue to keep tabs on their ex. It's Facebook stalking, and it's not good for you. I encourage you to de-friend and move on.

And why are we obsessed with having more and more friends? Does being able to display a long friend list give us some type of self-confidence? Sometimes it's funny to see if someone will accept a friend request after meeting once or twice. This is fairly common, yet I find it interesting. How is it that you become friends after a couple of encounters? Is it like a coffee machine—you press "start" and the friendship starts brewing? It's entertaining to observe how we use social media to create "friendships."

I think Facebook uses the word "friend" very loosely, and so I wonder if all of those people on your friend list are, in fact, friends. Included in your inventory may be some family members, co-workers, and childhood friends, as well as people you met at a conference or while on vacation. That is what's great about Facebook—you can build a social network and use it to stay in touch. However, it's important to find a healthy way to use it. If you log on to find out what friends are doing instead of contacting them, you may have a problem. Similarly, if you're using Facebook to chronicle every moment of your day, then you need to step away from the computer or mobile device and walk back into your own life.

You may also encounter a situation in which someone constantly tries to "friend" you, and you ignore the request and/or say no, but the person persists. Why? After I friend someone, I'll know whether or not she accepted my request within a couple of days. Some may take a week or two, but after three weeks or so, it's clear the request was not accepted. You can ponder why the person denied you a Facebook friendship, or realize that maybe the person doesn't think of you as a friend. Harsh, yes, but have you been in a situation when someone has sent you a request and you have no idea who the person is? Attaching a message to the request would be helpful. If you're trying to friend someone who may not know who are you, is that not a clue that maybe you two are not friends?

When someone keeps sending you friend requests, think about how you want to handle it. If ignoring leads to feelings of guilt, you could friend the person just to stop the madness. Another option would be to send the person a message explaining why you're denying her request; however, that seems like a lot of effort, and even somewhat mean. This is what technology has come to: a world full of high-school behaviors that we're still dealing with as adults. When will it end?

Situation 4: Birthdays on Facebook

Birthdays are wonderful occasions, celebrated with cake, candles, and presents. However, the Facebook version of birthdays is bizarre. The fact that Facebook reminds you of someone's birthday is great. When I had a birthday in August, it was interesting to see which friends posted a message on my wall that day and which did not. Many factors complicate this—for example, some people don't log on to their Facebook account every day, so they may not have known it was my birthday. But if you're really good friends with someone, you should already know when her birthday is, so relying on Facebook to remind us about someone's birthday is another issue.

Another interesting phenomenon to observe is who posts a comment instead of calling, e-mailing, or sending a birthday card (electronically or otherwise). I find it amusing that those who post comments, even though it's sweet and nice of them, are people I usually don't talk to on the other 364 days of the year. I'm not trying to destroy or minimize the celebration of birthdays, but during my last Facebook birthday experience, I was bothered by the fact that out of roughly 400 friends, only about forty commented. That's quite sad. And what's even worse is to see who posts nice birthday messages on the walls of friends who have birthdays on the days before and after mine—and many of them didn't post on mine. I sound like a child crying because her piece of pizza is smaller than the next girl's, but this is what Facebook causes—high school drama and feelings of unworthiness. Unless your friends have set their security controls to the highest levels, you can see their posts, as well as live feeds, so it can be somewhat upsetting to see friends' posts on other friends' walls and no acknowledgement of your birthday. This can lead to hurt feelings, and there's no way to handle them gently because you can't say anything without sounding a bit crazy. For example, saying something like, "I can't believe you wrote on Erin's wall and not on mine on my birthday" may not go over well, regardless of age.

Birthdays are meant to be celebrated and acknowledged, and that's why we spend millions of dollars on them every year. We want our friends and loved ones to feel special as we celebrate their presence on this earth. All I ask is that, when it comes to birthdays, let's be a bit more aware.

These four common examples lead to one conclusion: be considerate, mature and responsible when using Facebook and how you post information. If you are and you utilize these qualities when using Facebook, then some of these issues may not apply to you. If you carelessly post about all the fun you're having and don't think about anyone else's feelings, then the words "considerate, mature, and responsible" do not come to mind. Therefore, some of these issues could be avoided if there was more thinking about how your actions affect others. That's all.

Women's Experiences and Thoughts About Facebook

I have come to question my use of Facebook, and have considered deleting my account. I often feel worse after logging on and seeing what my friends are up to; I'm usually left feeling like my life is not as exciting or worthwhile. This reminds me of an incident that occurred as I was writing this chapter. My friend Lisa—the one who's well beyond her years in wisdom—sent an e-mail to her family and friends to let everyone know she was saying goodbye to Facebook. After discussing this with her, and understanding her reasons for wanting real connection and communication, I've been wondering what my life would be like without Facebook.

At any rate, Lisa made a conscious decision last year to break ties with Facebook for good. She shares with me that it wasn't an easy decision to make, as most everyone is now on Facebook. However, Lisa says that she and Facebook weren't a good match. She enjoys her small, but very close, network of friends—and found that her Facebook friends didn't provide genuine feelings of connection. Even though these Facebook friends represented aspects of her life, such as college and various jobs, there was no connection beyond those shared experiences.

Lisa came to question what Facebook meant to her, as well as the meaning of "friend" on it. She also speculated about the superficial friendships that Facebook offers, and felt her other friendships suffered due to the ridiculous amounts of time people spend on it. In addition, she felt she became lazy about her friendships, because she was able to see her friends' status without having to call them. Out of her roughly one-hundred friends on Facebook, she talked to about thirty on a regular basis, meaning the remaining seventy were not part of her close circle of friends. It just wasn't enough for Lisa, and so she decided to delete her account.

Lisa sent the following e-mail to her family and friends, describing what she was doing and why.

> *I feel disconnected. I feel disconnected [from] my friends and family. Yes, yes, I have Facebook and LinkedIn, but at the end of the day I feel disconnected...I do not feel connected to you by reading your status updates on Facebook, or LinkedIn, or through Twitter (even though I don't use Twitter, it wouldn't help). And any other source of social media out there that claims to keep me in the loop with my friends and family [is] not helping! I realize that we are all busy, trust me, I know. I have even fallen to the allure of technology thinking "Oh, I checked on so-and-so's page, I know what's going on." The other day a friend and I were checking in and she asked, "Didn't you read my Facebook page?" So, this is me putting my foot down. I, a self-proclaimed phone caller, card writer/sender, e-mailer, and texter, [am] giving up Facebook. I miss the real*

connectedness I get when I hear a loved one's voice on the other end of the phone. I miss reading an amazing e-mail about my loved one's adventures or daily life routines. I need to hear the inflection in someone's voice when they share about a funny moment or the heartache of a loss or rejection. Yes, I miss my friends and family and nothing replaces them, but I will not settle for status updates as a way to feel connected. I will not continue to use lack of time as an excuse to show my friends and family that I am thinking/caring/missing/loving them.

So I say adieu, Facebook. May you forever keep people connected in your own special way as I do the same for me.

When I received this e-mail, I quickly shot Lisa a reply with my positive support and good wishes. She later told me she was somewhat worried about how her message would be interpreted. To her surprise, many of the responses were positive and supportive. Lisa felt good about the decision she'd made, and even more confident in her friendships. She has no idea what's happening with the rest of the people, and she's okay with that. She is keeping her good friends close in other ways, and that satisfies her just fine; plus, now she has more time to enjoy these friendships.

Lisa's story offers many lessons. First, I think she's brave for stepping away from Facebook and amazing for wanting real connections with the people in her life. Second, her story addresses all who use Facebook and how it may not be the best way to keep up with our friends except on a superficial level. Third, she truthfully addresses the number of friends some of us have on Facebook and whether they are, in fact, our "friends." I applaud Lisa and her decision.

Janice, who is in her fifties, says that of all the social media websites, she uses Facebook the least. She finds it too time consuming so she only uses it occasionally. Her children use Facebook more than she does. One positive Janice enjoys is finding old friends who are also on Facebook. However, she feels the process is similar to going to a reunion—you find out basic information, but nothing happens beyond that.

Callie, whom we met before, says she struggles with Facebook because she doesn't always understand the comments people post. I can understand this, as there is definitely some code of social conduct for interacting on Facebook. She is occasionally unsure if a comment is about her or not, and jokes that this is due partly to her personality.

Surviving Female Friendships: The Good, The Bad, and The Ugly
~ Nicole Zangara

She remembers a vague comment posted by a friend, and how she thought it was about her. Callie points out that many of her friends refuse to use Facebook at all.

Stacey, a woman in her twenties, has a very interesting outlook on Facebook and the Internet in general. Stacey remembers when her parents allowed her to have an AOL account when she was in middle school. She was delighted to have access to the web, and the freedom that comes with it. She spent her after-school time instant messaging her friends, and would sometimes go into teenage chat rooms that seemed appropriate and involved her interests and hobbies. Stacey's parents talked to her about setting boundaries, and had rules for her Internet use. It was all so new and exciting.

Stacey's parents emphasized that she was not to give out any personal information to anyone, under any circumstances, nor was she allowed to meet in person anyone she met online. She followed these rules accordingly. But Stacey says that having had these principles drilled into her as a child has resulted in a difficult internal struggle as an adult. She finds it unsettling that many people use Facebook and the Internet for almost everything now, because she still hears her parents telling her to be careful and to not share personal details.

Surviving Female Friendships: The Good, The Bad, and The Ugly
~ Nicole Zangara

Although she uses the web to make plans with friends and arrange dates, Stacey still feels somewhat odd about using the Internet for such things because of her parents' warnings. Her parents are still her parents, and their concerns still matter to her. She also says that she sometimes feels behind the times, and that she's missed out on potential friendships and romantic relationships due to her concerns. Stacey admits that she knows she needs to get on the bandwagon, but finds it somewhat unnatural.

Stacey's story illustrates a valid and legitimate argument about the Internet. As children, we're taught not to use the Internet to meet people; then we're force-fed Facebook and online dating sites, and are told to use them as a way to maintain and create friendships and romantic relationships when we're older. Confusing, right?

I agree with Stacey because I think that women of all ages are struggling with coming to terms with and understanding how to make and have friendships in a world filled with technology and social media. Are we supposed to be okay with all this stuff just because we're tech-savvy and have the newest iPhone? I think it takes time to get used to, and I appreciate and respect Stacey for sharing her internal struggles.

Surviving Female Friendships: The Good, The Bad, and The Ugly
~ Nicole Zangara

Abby, a woman in her thirties, has a Facebook story—one of betrayal, deceit, and secrecy. Abby met Natalie many years ago and their friendship went through all of the normal friendship phases. However, Abby found getting to know Natalie quite difficult because of her private nature. She soon learned there were topics that one didn't approach with Natalie—topics that friends discuss, like family, marriage, and work. But Abby felt Natalie had other positive qualities and enjoyed spending time going shopping or out to dinner with her.

Natalie met a man which Abby had suspicions about since Natalie's divorce proceedings began. Because of her attitudes about infidelity, Abby struggled with her feelings and didn't like Natalie's behavior. This is when the friendship began to take a turn for the worse. She saw Natalie change as she continued seeing Jake. He seemed controlling—not the type of man you would want your sister or daughter to date. However, when Abby met Jake, she liked him; he was funny and nice, but controlling, nonetheless.

Over time, Natalie called less, and soon the two women were seeing very little of each other. Abby happened to be on Facebook one day and saw that Natalie was engaged. She was shocked and upset that she'd had to learn this on Facebook; it would have been nice for Natalie to have shared this information with her in another, more personal way. The two finally spoke on the phone and Natalie told Abby they were planning a small wedding and explained that Abby wouldn't be invited. This stung Abby and made her realize how broken this friendship was.

Abby soon heard from Natalie again because she had some questions about her wedding plans; however, it was clear that Natalie didn't like any of Abby's suggestions or ideas. As the wedding drew closer, Abby had all but given up on what was left of the friendship.

On the night of Natalie's wedding, Abby found pictures posted on Facebook by friends whom Natalie had told her were not invited. She was infuriated and upset and, above all, felt deceived.

After much thought, Abby e-mailed Natalie to tell her that continuing the friendship was up to her, and that it was getting to be too difficult to manage alone. She received a response, but couldn't recall much of what it said. She says she skimmed it, in part because she was past caring about the friendship, and in part because it was painful to be on Facebook and see Natalie in her own photos. What does one do with all of these memories and constant reminders?

Natalie's lies kept being exposed as Abby saw more pictures on Facebook. It was at that point that Abby felt confident enough to de-friend Natalie and wipe out this toxic friendship. She has no regrets and feels she can now give more time and attention to her other friends who treat her with respect, dignity—and above all—honesty.

Examining Facebook

Facebook has the ability to make people feel bad about their lives. Reading such posts as, "Going skydiving!" "Packing for my ten-day trip to the Bahamas!" "Just ran five miles and feel great!" "Starting my vegan diet!" can cause you to compare yourself to others and feel that you're not measuring up. Some people post information as a way to boost their ego—and I wonder how they would do that without Facebook.

Most people don't post messages that are incriminating or make them seem evil; rather, they're often silly, positive, or a way to make themselves feel better. For example, have you ever read posts like these?

"Just got fired!"
"Just received a life sentence!"
"About to end my three-year marriage!"

You probably haven't read those kinds of posts. Why do people feel the need to boast on Facebook? Is it to feel superior or worthy of attention? Maybe I'm overanalyzing, but what is the point?

For women who tend to be jealous and feel insecure in female friendships, reading another friend's post can cause some self-esteem issues. Of course, not all women are insecure and think poorly of themselves; but there can be jealousy and competition in certain female friendships and Facebook magnifies these feelings.

And so the question becomes: what is Facebook's purpose? Sure, people use it to send out invitations, find old friends, and stalk people. So maybe the world would not end if I, too, stepped away from Facebook. I don't feel closer to any friend because of it. Truthfully, it simply annoys me and I know it can be a time-waster. I'd rather call a friend and ask how she's doing—and I don't need Facebook to do that. I'm not sure that giving up Facebook would be a sacrifice; I think it would help me connect with friends on a deeper level.

I do recognize that many individuals feel that Facebook is a great type of social media and that it can bring people together in uniquely positive ways. Jenny, most of whose friends are in New York City, finds that Facebook gives her a feeling of connection by reading her friends' updates or looking at their pictures.

Women can keep tabs on their children and grandchildren through Facebook and can also reconnect with people from their past. Lindsay, a woman in her sixties, enjoys finding people from her past. She's able to see where they are in their lives and what they're doing now. She also enjoys being reminded of friends' birthdays and anniversaries so she can send good wishes. Additionally, as a grandmother, Lindsay can see pictures of her children and grandchildren online.

However, I question why we're moving towards communication via wall posts; it seems impersonal and a little strange. Perhaps I need to post more often or post about mundane things. But I'd rather tell a friend about my experience, and allow a conversation to take place.

Even though Facebook can be a great tool to communicate and connect with friends, we're relying on it too much to create and maintain our social networks. As seen in Lisa's story, she didn't feel Facebook was providing any benefits so she walked away. In a sense, she had a breakup with Facebook—and I'd say she won. Similarly, Abby's story shows what can happen when a friend is not honest and how Facebook can provide the truth.

Surviving Female Friendships: The Good, The Bad, and The Ugly
~ Nicole Zangara

Maybe by the time this work is completed, I will have deleted my account—or at the very least—completed a friend inventory cleanse. Ultimately, I cannot win the fight against Facebook. But, I can control how I use it and to what extent. I challenge you to think about Facebook and the Internet in general. It's important to not only communicate with our friends, but to also take a close look into how we go about doing it.

ഇ Chapter Eleven രു

Technology, Connection, and Miscommunication

*T*echnology is amazing; and how it's transformed the ways in which we communicate over the last ten to twenty years is even more fascinating. I didn't have a cell phone until college. Well, I had a car cell phone in high school, but was only allowed to use it for emergencies. When I got my first hand-held cell phone, I thought it was the most spectacular thing I'd ever seen. I never turned it off, and constantly played around with the ring tones. As technology advanced, I got newer and sleeker cell phones with more features. Now my phone flips to a keyboard, which makes sending text messages much easier since I have space to press the keys instead of trying to type using the number pad.

161

Surviving Female Friendships: The Good, The Bad, and The Ugly
~ Nicole Zangara

I find technology interesting because, superficially, we feel connected because we have an overwhelming number of ways to connect—Facebook and Twitter; texting, calling, or Skyping. But is it connecting or just staying in touch? E-mails and texts are ways to connect, but if that's our only form of communication (unless we see each other on a more frequent basis), isn't that rather shallow? I've often heard people say, jokingly, "That's my e-mail friend," or "She and I are texting buddies." Maybe I'm behind the times, but I find it nice to have a conversation—either on the phone or in person. Texting and typing can be tiring; besides, written messages can sometimes be misinterpreted. It's easier to make a point with a phone call or, better yet, in person. How many times have you or a friend read a text or e-mail and had a negative reaction? Maybe that wasn't the intention, but you read the words literally when they were meant to be sarcastic or a joke. Many times, words transmitted through technology can be taken in a different or negative way, and misunderstandings occur due to these miscommunications.

For example, a friend texts you and accidentally adds an exclamation point where there should have been a question mark. "What's your problem!" versus "What's your problem?" reads very differently. Or a friend accidentally

162

texts you something that she meant to text her mother or sister, and you're confused whether it was meant for you in the first place. If you have friends who have the same first letter, such as Carly and Caroline, you may send a text to Carly that was meant for Caroline if you're not paying attention to who you select from your contact list. Another example is when a friend misspells a word or two and you attempt to interpret the message, and it may not be what she intended.

Miscommunications can also occur because if you're not constantly checking your cell phone, e-mail accounts, Facebook account, and/or Twitter account—to name but a few—then you may not be up to date on what's going on with your friends. But how are you supposed to be that connected? It's hard to know everything that's going on unless you have the time and energy to devote to doing so. For example, I once had a friend text and e-mail me the same information, and I was stumped about how to reply. Should I e-mail or text her back? Is the information so important that it has to be sent via two or three modes?

You don't have to call a friend about everything since texting can be sufficient if you're figuring out a time and place to meet. But when you text back and forth, do the accumulated messages seem like essays? I'm guilty of doing this instead of just calling, so I put myself in this category. I want to understand why we do this. Has using our voices and conversing become obsolete?

What is limiting about these modes of communication is that they don't always allow a conversation to happen. It seems that we've lost the ability to make a phone call, to take that extra step to reach out because we have so many other, easier ways of communicating. Think about the last time you texted a friend. Maybe the back-and-forth took a day, because both of you responded when you had time. Yes, that's considered a conversation, but would it have been easier to have had it over the phone? Was the topic important enough to speak about? Maybe it was simpler and worth the texting, but I wonder how much more effort a phone call would've taken and if there would've been the same outcome or feeling of connection.

Personally, I enjoy hearing my friend's laughter or, better yet, seeing her expressions and mannerisms. Reading "LOL" in an e-mail or text is nice, and I'm happy to know she's laughing, but it's not the same; I'd rather be laughing with my friend. Have you ever been in a room full of women who were laughing? Laughter is so contagious that it's hard not to chuckle yourself—even if you have no idea what they're laughing about. Or sometimes you exchange a look with a friend and you both start laughing like hyenas. These are the beautiful moments when words aren't needed—sometimes all it takes is a look or a gesture. These shared experiences bring friends closer and build inside jokes; an e-mail or text won't because you can't explain it over e-mail or text. Have you tried? It's impossible. This is where words alone are not enough—you need that human interaction.

Furthermore, when a friend calls you crying or wanting to discuss her horrible day, you hear the pain and sorrow in her voice. Sharing that phone call is important because you're connecting with her and you're present with her. It's difficult to see a friend crying, but I know how it feels when you're crying and your friend is willing to sit with you and be there. An e-mail or text can't give you a hug or wipe away your tears.

We depend so heavily on our cell phones that we forget technology can fail us. We think that we'll always be able to connect somehow. I learned this lesson the hard way during Hurricane Ike in September, 2008. I had just moved to Houston, Texas and, ironically, added texting to my cell phone plan. After the storm, I wasn't able to make any phone calls, and texting was iffy. I soon came to realize how disconnected I felt, as well as feeling lonely and scared. On the second night, a coworker who had stayed with me the first night went back to her place because her electricity had been restored. That night felt like the longest of my life. My cell phone battery was low, so I turned it off and tried to sleep. I was hot and tired, and the silence was deafening. I never felt so alone in my life. I was without my family, friends, utilities and I couldn't make a phone call or send a text. I cried and felt like crap. Thanks, Hurricane Ike.

The next day, as power started to come back on, I drove to a local hardware store and charged my cell phone. When I was finally able to make a successful phone call, I was relieved and excited to hear my family members' voices. Simple phrases felt like a million hugs and I instantly felt better. Of course, being around other people who were also charging their cell phones helped, too. Connection is incredibly powerful; we need to feel a connection to others, as these are basic needs of human nature.

Have you ever been out to dinner with a friend who keeps checking her cell phone? Or maybe you're guilty of this. It's rude and can interfere with the human connection you're having with your friend. We need someone to say, "Put the cell phones away," much like how the airlines handle it when you're on an airplane. After landing, musical tones fill the cabin when everyone turns their cell phones on and starts making phone calls. I always wonder who they're calling—and if it's really important? Instead of worrying about checking our cell phones, it would be nice to enjoy a meal with a friend so you remember how the connection feels.

I think that's one reason to go on vacation—it encourages you to be inaccessible. Have you ever heard a friend say that she was taking a vacation and planned to not check her work e-mail? It's as if the word "vacation" gives us an excuse to disconnect. Or that same friend tells you that she may not turn on her laptop at all and just have a staycation (a stay-at-home vacation)? It's fascinating that we set rigid boundaries when it comes to vacations because we can't set boundaries with our mobile devices in our daily lives. I realize not all of us do this and that some of you put your cell phone on silent or even turn it off at times, but the majority of us use it like an extension of ourselves.

Another situation I find amusing is texting back and forth with a friend, when her messages suddenly stop with no warning that she had to go to the bathroom or into a meeting—nothing. I'm not glued to my cell phone all day, but these experiences confuse me. What happened? I'm baffled when someone stops texting without follow up. Or have you texted someone and not received a response for two or three days? Call me old fashioned, but when someone contacts me, I try to respond within twenty-four hours. It's a lesson in common courtesy that I learned from my parents and feel strongly about. If the person is unable to respond, I can and will respect that; however, when we're all easily accessible, connected, and constantly checking our mobile devices, it's hard to believe it can take that much time to receive a response. Moreover, some people keep their cell phone next to them at all times, so it's difficult to believe they didn't get your text or call. The next time you call, e-mail, or text someone, see how long it takes for her to get back to you; same with someone contacting you. These are behaviors we should be aware of.

Another point about technology is for those of you who feel more comfortable texting and talking on the phone versus human interaction. I empathize, because I think we're becoming more comfortable with maintaining relationships through technology rather than face-to-face contact. Many write e-mails because we feel more secure than exchanging information in person. It depends on the type of person you are; if you're shy, you may prefer to reach out over the phone rather than in person.

We're acclimating to technology, as a lot of our contact throughout the day is through some form of it. For

168

example, now we can talk to the latest iPhone and it will give us a verbal response. The idea that we're creating relationships with technology is bizarre and fascinating at the same time; yet there's still a need for human contact and connection—and there always will be.

Friendships need to be cared for. Technology is great for fostering them and reaching out, but what about picking up the phone if the topic of conversation is important and meaningful? Think back to some of your best friendship memories. Are they made up of texting, or of having a blast at a concert? Are they memories of leaving a voicemail or of taking a road trip? My guess is that you remember the experiences. A cell phone can't provide that.

As in the last chapter, the take-away message here is to be considerate, mature, and responsible—as well as being aware of your behavior. If you're with a friend and she's spending half the time on her cell phone, ask her if something is wrong. Similarly, if you're out with a friend and you're more entertained by your cell phone, maybe it's time to re-evaluate your friendship.

As technology keeps advancing, it will be interesting to see how communication continues to evolve.

Lindsay: A Woman in Her 60s

Lindsay has experienced a pattern in her female friendships—her best friends turn out not to be. Lindsay says that there were people in her life she'd originally thought were her best friends; and she was sure the friendships would last a lifetime. They didn't. She shares two of her experiences with me in the following story:

Lindsay and Amber became friends after Lindsay relocated, and remained so for about eighteen years. Coincidentally, Amber had just moved to the same area, so they were in the same situation, and both of them had young children. Looking back, Lindsay sees how unhealthy this friendship was, but again, hindsight is always 20/20.

The two women would talk for hours, work out, and engage in other social activities together. They talked and complained about their husbands and children and the challenges of both; they held nothing back. They had so much in common and so much to talk about

The friendship continued when Lindsay got divorced, and Amber continued to complain about her husband and how unhappy she was in her marriage. She discussed leaving her husband and, at the same time, spoke about her infidelities. When she finally left the marriage, Amber focused on finding another man and discussed it all with Lindsay. After finding someone on an online dating site, Amber moved to live with him but the two still kept in contact.

A few months went by before Amber told Lindsay she was planning to end her relationships and cut ties with everyone in the town she was from—except for a few people. Then, Amber's son got engaged; Lindsay was invited to the wedding and said she'd be there. On the day of the wedding, Lindsay's fiancé was ill, experiencing chest pains. She called Amber to tell her she wouldn't be able to attend the wedding. Amber was angry and refused to speak to her.

The two women had a mutual friend and Lindsay attempted to apologize through him, but it didn't lead to anything positive. This friend then told Lindsay that Amber was angry because she hadn't wanted to invite her to the wedding in the first place, and was even angrier that she had to pay for their unused seats. Lindsay offered to pay Amber back, but the message she received from the mutual friend was that Amber had never thought of Lindsay as a friend, and that her son hated her and was relieved that she didn't attend the wedding. They have not spoken since then. Lindsay still can't believe what happened and continues to feel the pain of Amber's feelings about the friendship.

Lindsay had another negative experience with Carol, whom she met during law school. They were very close and spoke every day. Lindsay thought they shared many similarities and had a lot in common. Even though Carol was younger, the friendship seemed good. Carol was fun, smart, and enjoyable to be around. The two participated in law journal during their second year, and both ran for election as editors for the following year. Carol won and became chief editor; Lindsay was a staff editor, yet she looked forward to working with Carol.

Without any warning or explanation, however, Carol stopped talking to Lindsay. She clearly remembers walking into Carol's office to find out what was going on; Carol said she couldn't talk about it and cried. Lindsay told Carol that whatever it was, she hoped Carol could tell her, and she would be there for her when that time came. She also apologized in the event she had done something wrong and, if she had, promised that she would try to fix it. The time never came and the two never talked again. Lindsay recounts this experience as one that still confuses her and leaves her speechless.

I also had an interesting discussion with Lindsay about her definition of friendship. I asked her what qualities she would expect in a friend. She feels that true friends are rare and hard to find—and they only exist in fiction. Lindsay believes that a true friend is someone who leaves you feeling better, but will be honest about her thoughts and feelings in a respectful way. She also believes that a true friend is someone who is your biggest ally and toughest critic. When discussing these qualities, Lindsay says that person should be your husband or loved one, your children or parents; but then realizes that a friend is someone who loves you even though you're not related and the feelings are mutual. Lindsay believes that a true friendship is one in which you're there for each other even though you have different lives.

After discussing these qualities, Lindsay admitted that she has a fairytale idea of what a friend is supposed to be. Are these descriptions fairytale-esque? I don't believe so; they describe a healthy, solid friendship. So why are they so hard to find and maintain?

⅏ Chapter Twelve ⅍

Letting Go

*T*his last chapter may seem somewhat sad, but my goal is for you to look at your friendships and be honest about how they make you feel. I hope you gain some insight into looking at those around you, as well as a better understanding of yourself.

Before I go any further, it's important to note that I do believe recovery is possible in a friendship, yet it takes both people to make the repair happen. It requires being honest and open about your feelings, as well as validating each other's perspectives. If you both are able to heal the wounds through developing a new appreciation and understanding, then the friendship can continue, be successful, and survive. Many friends are able to discuss a conflict or repair the damage when both people value the friendship and want it to work. That is the key: that both people care enough about the friendship not to let it go, and in a way, to fight for its survival. Recovery can take place; yet, if it's clear you're fighting solo, you may need to take a second look at the friendship.

Janice, whom we met earlier, shared her friendship breakup story with me. She believes that women can connect and come together easily when there is a powerful chemistry. She even calls this "love at first sight," because it's effortless. In other instances, however, Janice believes we sometimes outgrow friendships, but it's difficult to end them. Her story illustrates this.

Janice was sixteen years old when she met Danielle on a teen trip to Europe. They had a wonderful time together, as well as a powerful chemistry, and Janice believed this friendship would last a lifetime. She describes her and Danielle as "two peas in a pod" who shared so many similarities that they talked nonstop for the entire eight weeks of the trip. Fortuitously, they both lived only about twenty minutes from each other in New Jersey. So, when they returned home from the trip, they were able to continue the friendship and spend as much time together as possible. They talked about their goals, their dreams, and their boyfriends, among many, many other things. The two understood each other and were inseparable.

Surviving Female Friendships: The Good, The Bad, and The Ugly
~ Nicole Zangara

Danielle told Janice that she imagined her getting married and having the white-picket-fence fairytale, complete with two-and-a-half kids and a dog; Danielle thought she would not. And she was right. It became clear to Janice that the two were following very different paths which didn't intersect at any point. They grew apart, as often happens when two women become independent and mature.

Janice says that she wanted out of the friendship, yet Danielle held on tightly. Janice found this very difficult, so she first tried avoidance and then began to make excuses. When she moved across the United States, she thought it was her way out—an easy, clean break. But Danielle moved to the same city. Yes, really.

When Janice had her first child, Danielle came to visit. At the end of that get-together, Janice knew it was time to talk and also knew it wasn't going to be pretty. It was clear to Janice how different they'd become, and not addressing it only made it more awkward.

Janice says that by this time, the friendship was so far gone that they no longer had anything in common. She prepared herself for the talk, and knew it was now or never. Janice still feels uncomfortable about that conversation; it was difficult for both of them. And she learned that there's no easy way to end a friendship.

Surviving Female Friendships: The Good, The Bad, and The Ugly
~ Nicole Zangara

Nancy, whom we also met earlier, was on the receiving end of a friendship breakup many years ago. Although she's had to create distance in friendships, she doesn't remember ever ending one herself; so having it happen to her was a very challenging experience because she'd put so much into this particular relationship.

Nancy and Lauren were good friends. Due to the nature of their close bond, Nancy had even opened up and let herself be vulnerable with Lauren, who then used what Nancy had said in a very hurtful and vindictive way. For example, Lauren started doing things with other women that they used to do together. Nancy began to feel insecure about the friendship, and she shared her feelings with Lauren. Lauren then turned it around and made Nancy feel that she was the bad person for feeling this way. She remembers how she was put down and accused by Lauren instead of feeling empathy from her. The two never spoke again.

Nancy is able to look back on what happened with Lauren and say that it was one of the best things that could've happened to her. At that time in her life, Nancy didn't have a large network of friends and this breakup forced her to make new ones. She soon realized that she'd put too much into this one friendship without getting anything in return. She was able to let her anger go by

177

acknowledging that she had very little control over the situation, and that it may have had very little to do with her. Nancy also says that Lauren didn't understand her, and now sees that the friendship was very unhealthy. She was able to realize that she was handed a golden opportunity to reach out to other women who were understanding and healthy. For Nancy, what started off as a painful loss resulted in a lasting gain that is still paying off in positive ways.

It can be challenging to end a friendship, especially if you're on the receiving end. Even though positives sometimes come out of these situations, they may not be evident for some time. If you, however, want to breakup, it's difficult to decide how to do it. Additionally, you may question whether it's time to end the friendship or if you should give it time, and then return to it later when both parties have had time to think and/or grow.

These questions need to be asked, especially when trying to handle a fragile friendship that was once a very strong bond. Many people avoid these inquiries because they're difficult questions that require reflection, and they make us look at ourselves and the other person and ask, "Now what?" And ending a friendship isn't an easy decision to make because we often don't want to end things or let them go.

Moreover, if we have a long history with a friend, we've most likely shared very personal thoughts and/or feelings and felt comfortable doing it at the time, but now wonder what that person will do with the information. As petty as that sounds, females can quickly turn from nurturing to vicious when feeling attacked since there is an innate need to protect ourselves. There may be words exchanged that seem scary, because you'll always wonder if that person will keep your confidences or use them against you; moments we wish we could take back. If there is conflict when a friendship ends, lingering fears about what may happen to intimate exchanges are common.

Do you remember the old adage, *Keep your friends close and your enemies closer*? I can't tell you how many times I've heard people say it jokingly, but do just that as a way of keeping tabs on a frenemy so they know what she's up to. Do we want to have someone in our lives whom we consider an enemy (or frenemy) for no other purpose than to keep up with her latest scheme? If you can't stand someone, why stay friends? I ask you to consider all your friendships and ask yourself if there are any frenemies among them. If so, what's the point of the friendship? I'm always surprised to hear people's reasons, as if they're getting something out of the relationship; for example, "She always gets into the best clubs/parties/restaurants," or, "She's friends with my boyfriend/husband." I understand that certain situations require us to be friendly with other females; however, I question keeping around people for reasons that seem, well, silly.

Our fears may get in the way of ending a friendship; fears of being alone, of getting older and wondering who will come to our big life events (weddings and funerals). If you're single, friends and family probably form your main support systems, and the last thing we want is to lose those we consider most important. Also, as we age, we think more about our identity and about mortality. Fear, so common in friendships, can immobilize us and make our knees buckle, but it's not the best reason for holding on to a friendship, especially if it's time to let it go. Therefore, you may need to ask yourself some tough questions about why you're holding on to certain friends.

I consider myself a Type A personality, so letting a friendship go seems like a failure. When you've had several negative friendship experiences, it can become an "another one down the drain" mentality when a friendship doesn't work out or hits a rough patch. It's difficult not to take it personally and wonder what it is about you that creates these outcomes.

Surviving Female Friendships: The Good, The Bad, and The Ugly
~ Nicole Zangara

I've experienced these feelings, and they can be a hit to your self-esteem. Now, when I meet someone new, I sometimes doubt the potential for a friendship because of past hurts and negative friendship experiences. This can cause self-doubt, and you may be reluctant to try again. Remember the emotional baggage I referred to earlier? That's me, carrying all my baggage into this new friendship, and it's not doing anyone any good. Similarly, when a relationship breaks up, many women will say, "I never want to date again!" After a breakup (friendship or romantic), feelings are raw and overwhelming. It's okay to take a break; however, it's important not to give up entirely and/or feel guilty.

Esther, whom we also met earlier, told me that she feels she has failed at friendships. When I asked her why and how, she said that when she logs onto Facebook and sees long-lasting friendships, she thinks something is wrong with her. She sees her friendship breakups as her failures because she has a difficult time believing that other people have flaws; she believes it was something she did which caused a friendship breakup or that she could have done something to prevent it.

Esther sometimes thinks she should have been more flexible and understanding, but knows now that she really couldn't have done anything other than what she did. Looking back on many of her friendships, she realizes they were one-sided and unhealthy. She was always drawn to those with a fun, dramatic, free-spirited outlook; she was the grounded one to whom they came for support and guidance. When Esther was in need of help, these people weren't there for her. Esther is grateful for the friends she has now, because they are there for her—with open arms.

It's safe to assume that people who care about their friendships would feel some sense of disappointment if they have to face a friendship ending. Also, letting a friendship go can trigger negative feelings and recall painful past experiences—the emotional baggage. Even though the situation may be out of our hands, we feel a sense of responsibility when we lose a friend. Not only do we lose the friendship, but we also lose a connection to happy moments. It can be way too easy to internalize these feelings and feel as though you've failed. As women, we're generally hard on ourselves, so I challenge you to not go there in your mind. However, I realize it's easier said than done.

There's an accumulation of shared experiences in a friendship as well as mementos we hold onto as ways to re-experience and remember. Also, we may have played a major role in a friend's happy life event, so there's additional pain and sadness when recalling those occasions. Some friends have said that they wish they could Photoshop their now ex-friends out of their wedding pictures because of negative experiences they have had with the people in the pictures post-wedding. The sudden realization that we will not have happy moments with them again makes reminders painful. It's important to acknowledge all the feelings that can get stirred up when facing a friendship breakup.

For that reason, it is crucial to grieve the friendship. This may sound silly, but it needs to happen. Get a group of your friends together, and ask them about ex-friends or friendships they've had to let go. It may be surprising to hear the stories and the responses. We all go through these situations and it's helpful to know that others have experienced similar occurrences.

There's no right or wrong way to grieve a friendship. Breaking up with a friend is equally, if not more, difficult than breaking up with a romantic partner. Female friendships often provide deeper connections than those with a male friend or a romantic partner. There's a type of understanding between women; and the ability to love, nurture, and care often come to the forefront in a female relationship. Therefore, going through the grieving process is essential to understanding yourself and the friendship.

Surviving Female Friendships: The Good, The Bad, and The Ugly
~ Nicole Zangara

As we get older, we see our friends differently—and vice versa—which may impact the friendship. We may look at their actions and decisions through different eyes and need to talk with them about these perceptions. Friendships may become more difficult as we mature because our friends may take a job we don't think will suit them or they may date someone we think is a jerk. Worse yet, they may marry that person, and then we have to figure out how we're going to manage the friendship as well as our honest thoughts and feelings. Many friendships fail due to a lack of honesty (not brutal honesty) and being too timid to speak up for fear the friend will get upset and/or leave. So the question is, do we say something or keep our mouths shut? The latter, I've found, leads to resentment—which is detrimental to any friendship.

If friends are able to be honest and open, there will be less miscommunication and fewer misunderstandings. The person may not like what you have to say, but the two of you may be better off for having had the conversation than letting issues linger. If the problem can't be resolved, taking a break or letting the friendship go are options. Again, this is not easy to discuss; but if the friendship is meaningful to both of you, it's important to address the concerns. You and your friend may view it as a sabbatical, as needed space. Or, you may need, at that time or later, to redefine the relationship and each of your expectations. If both people come into the conversation with open minds and non-defensive language and behavior, the conversation may be easier than you think. If that doesn't work, then maybe it's time to rethink the friendship and how you see this person in your life. Some people would rather let the friendship run its course than discuss what's happening. That may work in the short-term, but what good is avoidance in the long-term? There's a possibility that similar issues will occur again in another friendship, and so they need to be addressed sooner than later.

Saying goodbye to a friend seems somewhat unnatural. However, giving a friendship a proper farewell may be essential to moving on and having closure. That may mean that you write a letter to the person and then rip it up. Or you could collect pictures and other memorabilia and put them in a box, and then store that box in a closet or a place where it's out of sight; or, if you're feeling really angry, simply throw it away. The process will be different depending on the nature of the friendship as well as how it ended. It's important to address the value of the friendship and what it meant to you over the years. It will be a painful process, yet it will allow you to cherish the memories and experiences from a different perspective instead of with rage and disappointment.

We often avoid being angry and/or hurt instead of realizing where the feelings are coming from; they can be unresolved emotions from past experiences. Many women have a difficult time expressing their anger because, culturally, we are taught not to. So when something happens with a friend, it can be difficult to acknowledge the anger and stop it from overpowering us. That's why it's crucial to grieve and to allow yourself to feel all of the accompanying emotions—anger included—so you can let it go.

If the friendship didn't end on good terms, it can be difficult to grieve without anger and resentment towards the person. When we really can't stand the person, we may find ourselves wanting to say mean things about her or broadcast her secrets—but that only causes major damage and it certainly won't make things better. Would you want her to share your secrets? Finding healthy ways to express your anger may be hard, but will provide valuable life lessons.

Anger is a powerful emotion that, if not adequately worked through, can become a barrier to future friendships. We all know what anger feels like and how it can feel to be around angry people. If we're able to work through our anger, we may come to appreciate the friendship for what it was, as well as what it provided us, during that time in our lives. For me, there have been some friendships that ended badly or ended without explanation, yet I've found that, with (a lot of) time and (a lot of) space, I've come to a better understanding of the person. I may not have understood why the friendship ended, or liked and/or agreed with what happened. Rather, I believe that friends come in and out of our lives for different reasons, and sometimes we have to accept the terms—good or bad. Acceptance can be incredibly challenging if you're still feeling hurt and angry, but it will come with time. However, some friendships end so badly that acceptance may never be possible. But sometimes we have to look at the positives of the friendship, even when they don't outweigh the negatives, in order to let our negative feelings go. It is a choice we have to make. Do we continue feeling angry or do we decide to focus on our other friends and redirect that energy? It's up to you to decide how and when to move forward in the best possible way you can.

Nothing lasts forever and there are no guarantees in life, especially regarding human behavior. Diamonds last forever; friendships do not. We sometimes outgrow our relationships or we take different paths; we may make decisions our friends don't agree with, and vice versa; we may move and find that the friendship just fizzles out. It's not good or bad, it just is. Therefore, for friendships to survive, we have to appreciate who we have in our lives now instead of who is not in our lives. I believe that if we can adopt this mentality, we'll feel more settled in our friendships and hopefully make better decisions about who we choose to be our friends. Sometimes we have to be grateful for what is, not what or how it should be.

As we get older and possibly meet our Mr. or Ms. Right, having a solid base of friends will help us through life's ups and downs. I don't regret any of my past friendships, even those that ended on bad terms. I don't regret my college experiences or being in a sorority because it allowed me to share in some wonderful occasions. I think that if I could go back, I would've told my recruitment class how I felt which may have opened the door to change; however, what-if discussions aren't helpful and don't alter a thing. For this reason, I'm thankful I had these experiences because each one taught me about myself, how to speak up for what I believe in, and how to be a better and more patient person. I believe each friendship is a journey and learning experience; even though we don't know the outcome, it's worth the ride, bumps and all.

❧ Epilogue ☙

$\mathcal{I}$n closing, I include a positive story of female friendship as well as a poem my mother gave me many years ago. It has meant a great deal to me and has helped me to navigate my own friendships. I like to reread the poem from time to time as it gives me perspective on what is important—as well as *who* is important—in my life.

Enjoy.

Alexandra: A Woman in Her 60s

Alexandra's story is about a longtime friend named Talia. When Alexandra thinks of the word *friend*, she thinks of Talia, the woman with whom she has been friends for over forty years. The two confide in each other and Alexandra has immense trust in and respect for Talia. They live far away from each other, but that doesn't stop them from picking up the phone or sending an e-mail.

What Alexandra remembers most about this friendship is how Talia has been there through some major ups and downs. When Alexandra had her first child, Talia and her husband came to the hospital and brought flowers to celebrate the new addition to their family. When times got financially tough for Talia, Alexandra was there, ready and willing to help in any way she could. Their friendship never wavered.

When Alexandra's husband became ill and then passed away, Talia was by her side, reassuring her and providing comfort and love. When both of Talia's children married, Alexandra was there to celebrate those happy, precious moments. Good times and bad, these two women have seen it all—together. When they're able to see each other, they reminisce about all their memories. To Alexandra, Talia is the definition of a friend.

Everyone Can't Be in Your Front Row
Author: Unknown

*L*ife is a theater. Invite your audience carefully. Not everyone is healthy enough to have a front-row seat in our lives. There are some people in your life that need to be loved from a distance.

It's amazing what you can accomplish when you let go, or at least minimize, your time with draining, negative, incompatible, not-going-anywhere relationships or friendships. Observe the relationships around you. Pay attention. Which ones lift and which ones lean? Which ones encourage and which ones discourage? Which ones are on a path of growth uphill and which ones are going downhill?

When you leave certain people, do you feel better or feel worse? Which ones always have drama, or don't really understand, know or appreciate you?

The more you seek quality, respect, growth, peace of mind, love and truth around you, the easier it will become for you to decide who gets to sit in the front row and who should be moved to the balcony of your life.

You cannot change the people around you.

But you can change the people you are around.

℘ About Nicole Zangara ℘

*N*icole Zangara has a Bachelor of Arts from American University in Washington, DC, and a Master of Social Work from Washington University in St. Louis. A licensed clinical social worker, she provides psychotherapy to people of all ages and backgrounds.

Born in Cambridge, Massachusetts and raised in Lexington, Nicole has lived in Washington, DC, St. Louis, and Houston, and now calls Arizona home where she moved to be closer to family. When she isn't working or writing, she enjoys traveling, hiking, and spending time with her family and friends.

CPSIA information can be obtained at www.ICGtesting.com
Printed in the USA
BVOW011106021212

307053BV00005B/26/P